Airbnb

How to Make a Six-Figure Income without Owning Any Property

Introducing...That ONE Thing That Will Make the BIGGEST Difference for Your Airbnb Business!!

I have something **exciting** to share with you! **IMAGINE** reaching your dreams and goals! This FREE bonus book reveals the hidden truth about mindset that most entrepreneurs do not know! Click on the link below **now** to discover that secret for yourself which has been **proven** effective for the most successful entrepreneurs! Get it now because you deserve to succeed!

http://bit.ly/SecretsForAirbnb

© Copyright 2018 - All rights reserved.

The content contained within this book may not be reproduced, duplicated or transmitted without direct written permission from the author or the publisher.

Under no circumstances will any blame or legal responsibility be held against the publisher, or author, for any damages, reparation, or monetary loss due to the information contained within this book. Either directly or indirectly.

Legal Notice:

This book is copyright protected. This book is only for personal use. You cannot amend, distribute, sell, use, quote or paraphrase any part, or the content within this book, without the consent of the author or publisher.

Disclaimer Notice:

Please note the information contained within this document is for educational and entertainment purposes only. All effort has been executed to present accurate, up to date, and reliable, complete information. No warranties of any kind are declared or implied. Readers acknowledge that the author is not engaging in the rendering of legal, financial, medical or professional advice. The content within this book has been derived from various sources. Please consult a licensed professional before attempting any techniques outlined in this book.

By reading this document, the reader agrees that under no circumstances is the author responsible for any losses, direct or indirect, which are incurred as a result of the use of information contained within this document, including, but not limited to, — errors, omissions, or inaccuracies.

Table of Contents

Introduction *10*

   What makes Airbnb unique? **11**

Chapter 1: Why Choose Airbnb? *14*

   Spacious and cost-effective.. 14
   Full kitchen.. 14
   Value proposition.. 15
   Neighborhood experience.. 16
   Social economics 16
   The financial benefits... 17
   Personal growth 17

Chapter 2: Things to Consider before You Embark on Your Airbnb Journey *19*

   Managing expectations.. 19
   Dealing with strangers.. 20
   Time constraints 21
   Unique listing.. 22
   Rapport with the landlords 22
   Interacting with neighbors 23
   Liability and risk exposure 23
   Setting the prices.. 24
   Adapting to the environment 24
   Necessary interruption 24
   Study and understand rental arbitrage........................ 25
   What are your goals? 25
   Understand the market... 26
   Insurance cover 27
   Business positioning 27

Chapter 3: Rental Arbitrage—How to Profit without Owning Any Property *28*

   How to go about rental arbitrage on Airbnb **29**

   What if the landlord says no? **31**

   How much will it cost?.. **32**

5

Airbnb projections for rental arbitrage 32

Risks involved in Airbnb arbitrage 33
    Regulations 34
    Market conditions 34
    Expect the unexpected 34

Chapter 4: Getting Permission from Landlords 36

Understand your landlord 37

Risks involved 38

Speaking to your landlord 39

Chapter 5: Market Research—an Important Step to Help Ensure Profitability 41

AirDNA 41
    Why do you need AirDNA? 42
    The AirDNA Mechanism 43
    Pricing strategy 44
    Identifying the competition 45

Factors that affect your listing 47
    Trip details 47
    Listing details 48
    Guest preferences 48
    Price 49
    Are you a Superhost? 49
    Reviews 49
    Helping new listings 49
    User experience 50
    Visibility 51

Chapter 6: Furnishing Your Airbnb 52

Functionality 52

Furniture form 53

Planning 55

Decorating guide for your Airbnb 56

Identify the target audience 56
Decorating your rental 57
Theme selection 58

Useful decoration tips 59
Color selection 59
Accent pieces 59
Context 60
Bed space 60
Spacious setting 60
Electrical outlets 61
Using doormats 61
Careful mirror placement 61
The living room 62
The bedroom 63

Chapter 7: Must Have Gadgets for Airbnb Hosts .. 65
Chargers 65
Entertainment 66
Media streaming device 66
Thermostats 66
Innovative lighting 67
Smart speakers 67
Programmable smart locks 68
Innovative doorbell 69
Security camera 70
Motion sensor 70
Airbnb insurance advice 70
Host Protection Insurance 71
Liability under the Airbnb insurance cover 72

Difference between Airbnb host guarantee and Airbnb host protection insurance 73
Airbnb cleaning fees 74
Property size 74
Type of property 75
Study the competition 75
Guest expectations 75
Hiring experts 76
Trial and error 76

Chapter 8: Listing Wizardry 78
Writing powerful descriptions 78
- Credible description 79
- Guest interaction 79
- Neighboring sights 80
- Airbnb ranking secrets 80
- Creating a standout listing 81
- A responsive host 81
- Reviews 82
- Wish lists 83

Airbnb pricing strategies 83
- Determine the target guest audience 84
- Hierarchical cost strategy 84
- Cost projections 85
- Shun desperation 85
- Guest demographics 86
- The type of property 86
- Study the competition 87

Optimizing your photos for maximum bookings 87
- Proper light setting 87
- Corner shots 88
- Detail in the photos 88
- Using panoramic shots 89
- Lifestyle photos 89
- Local sites 89
- Angular shots 90
- Aspect ratio and resolution 90

Chapter 9: Guest Relations 92

Messaging templates to communicate with guests 92

My rules, my house 94

Identifying problem guests before they book 96

Handling early arrivals and late checkouts 97

Dealing with Guest Cancellations 98

What to do if guests break something? 100

How to handle guests sneaking other people in 101

How to consistently get five-star experiences from guests 101

Chapter 10: Automating the Airbnb Process 104

Automated check-in 104

Using Airbnb management software 105
- Guest communication 105
- Managing multiple listings 106
- Schedule cleaning services 106
- Team management 107

Automation tools for Airbnb 108
- Auto message 108
- Automatic replies 108
- Automatic reviews 109
- Increasing efficiency as an Airbnb host 109
- Automatic sensors 110
- Automated emails 110

Chapter 11: Scaling It Up to Six Figures or More .. 112
- Winning mentality 113
- Importance of multiple listings 113
- Apt business mind-set 114
- Perfect imperfections 114
- Location choice 115
- Risk management 115
- Sound business plan 116

Chapter 12: Advanced Airbnb Tips 117

Save money on linens, towels, and sheets: How to prevent guests from staining your towels and sheets . 117
- How much should you pay your property managers? 117
- Advice on bedding and sheets 118

Conclusion 124

Introduction

In science, it has been said that the best way to study an animal is to witness its actions and interaction with its natural habitat. We can say the same thing about Airbnb, as the best way to interact with people and learn more about them and their local culture would be to interact with them and stay accommodated in their homes.

For an avid traveler, Airbnb offers an amazing opportunity to learn from new experiences, all the while saving money. Often, when you travel abroad, you check into a hotel, and it is always the same business environment. Checking into an Airbnb, however, allows you to experience a new country from the eyes of its own people. You can see the difference in their tasteful furniture, how things are arranged, the way they live, the decor and furniture types, and so forth. So what exactly is Airbnb?

Airbnb is a short-term accommodation service that means air, bed, and breakfast. It is a project that started in the year 2008, in response to the demand for accommodation when there was insufficient capacity to house the participants at a large conference in San Francisco. Today, the project has grown into a large company that offers accommodation in almost two hundred countries.

The concept of Airbnb is unique because the company itself does not own any lodging facility, just like Uber does not own any vehicles. What they do is create a connection between prospective guests and potential real estate property owners.

At the time of this writing, Airbnb has more than 2 million properties listed, and the number is growing every day.

What makes Airbnb unique?

One of the key reasons for the thriving of Airbnb is trust—it is a service platform that is essentially built on trust. The guest and the host trust that they will both conduct themselves in due diligence to make sure that they have a good time in the premise. To make yourself approachable and trustworthy, it is important to complete your profile, either as a guest or a host, and provide as much information about yourself as you deem necessary.

This information helps keep your profile credible and make it easier for the guest to be admitted into the host's property. Please remember that hosts have the right to reject a reservation request, especially if they are suspicious about the nature of a guest.

The Airbnb system is further boosted by automation systems and, together with mutual references shared by hosts and guests after their interaction, increases the level of credibility in the system.

Airbnb has gone a step further to weed out frauds, by limiting the possibility of contact between hosts and guests to the private message platform on Airbnb, as opposed to sharing personal contact details.

Just like with hotels, there are three types of rooms that you can find when you register on Airbnb:

- Shared rooms—this means that you will sleep on a bed or a sofa in a shared room.

- Private rooms—you get an entire room to yourself, which is the closest comparison to a hotel room.

- Entire apartment—this option allows you to rent the entire property, and you are free to use all equipment and amenities on the property unless otherwise stated.

Searching for a property on Airbnb is very simple. You indicate where you want to visit, the number of people who are visiting, and the number of nights you are checking into the property for. You can also take things a notch higher by indicating filters on things like the equipment you need in the premise, the size, location, price, type of room, and so on.

The cost of accommodation on Airbnb is broken down into the following:

- Room rate per night
- Cost of cleaning (determined by the host)
- Service fee
- Taxes where applicable

In some properties, hosts can request a security deposit. Where this applies, it will be indicated in the description of the property. Once the guest chooses their preferred room, the host receives the request and decides whether they approve or not.

The host is free to reject the request if the timing or profile of the guest does not suit their preference. When the host accepts the reservation, Airbnb deducts the total cost from the credit card, depositing funds in the Airbnb account until the guest arrives at the premise.

Also, some hosts have made instant booking available on their properties. This is a good way to accept reservations even when they are not around.

Chapter 1: Why Choose Airbnb?

There are many places where you could have chosen to stay for your holiday, but you chose Airbnb. A rental premise on Airbnb offers better value for the duration of your stay than checking into a hotel. If you are an adventurous traveler, you will appreciate Airbnb mostly because of the flexibility and the fact that you get to enjoy a homely stay.

What makes Airbnb stand out from all the other players in the short-term rental market? In value, Airbnb is worth more than $25 billion, competing closely with brands such as Marriott and Hilton.

Spacious and cost-effective

Having a lot of space is one of the reasons a lot of people prefer Airbnb to hotels or any other options, as it offers more space than you could find in any hotel room. Take the case of a family of five who are planning a holiday. In a hotel suite, the family would need two or three rooms. However, with Airbnb, the family can live under the same roof, with everyone getting their own bedroom in a three-bedroom apartment while paying less than they would in a hotel.

Full kitchen

Airbnb homes are fitted with full kitchens, which gives you room to prepare your meals just the way you like them. If needed, some homes even offer a chef on standby who will prepare hearty meals for you, down to your specifications. What this means is, you no longer have to worry about spending so much on takeout food and meals in hotels. During your Airbnb stay, you can eat as healthily and often as you do at home.

Value proposition

There is a lot more value for you in an Airbnb property than a hotel listing. Most rental properties have features that are not available in a hotel or which would cost you more if they were available. You can check into a home that has a canoe, bicycle, amazing home entertainment services, a private swimming pool, and family games like foosball and a pool table.

These are features that would cost you more in a hotel. Besides, most hotels will charge you more for a room with an ocean view, but in an Airbnb listing, you may have direct access to the beach for free, complete with secure lighting in case you want to visit the beach late at night.

Vacation rentals have a dryer and a washer, so you can travel as a family and only bring your carry-on luggage with you. During the stay, you can still do your laundry without worrying about additional costs. From the moment you book a reservation, consult the host to know about the amenities that they have in their premise, as this will help you reduce the number of things you bring in your luggage.

Neighborhood experience

Checking into an Airbnb is a good way to learn about neighborhoods in different parts of the world. In some communities, you will interact with diverse people, learn more about them, and even make new friends.

This is different from a hotel scenario that may be limited to tourist areas, which are all about spending money. Regarding aesthetics, Airbnb is a fun way to travel. The restaurants and shops in the neighborhoods are more affordable than what you would pay for food in a hotel, and the people you meet may even be happier and friendlier.

Most of the homeowners provide information that is more relevant and appropriate to you than the information that you will get from hotel staff. Hotel staff tends to recommend places where they can earn referral discounts, whether you enjoy the service or not. Homeowners, on the other hand, offer down-to-earth options for restaurants, authentic places where you can hang out, and their local favorites.

Having looked at some of the reasons Airbnb is a good fit for a guest, let's consider what a host stands to gain from using the service. For a digital hustler, Airbnb offers one of the best career paths. There are many challenges that you may experience when you are renting your premise, but in the long run, the benefits greatly outweigh the risks.

Social economics

A lot of people tend to focus on stories of bad Airbnb

experiences but rarely ever mention the good ones. There are so many people who have had an amazing experience on Airbnb, and they end up creating amazing, lasting relationships.

As a host, you will meet people from diverse parts of the world. They will endear you with stories from where they are from and share experiences, and some will even invite you to visit their country as a sign of good faith, in appreciation of how amazing of a host you are to them.

You get a deeper insight into life when you talk to someone from a different part of the world about their perspectives on life. Because of the way you interact with your guests, you make meaningful connections, personal and professional.

The financial benefits

Depending on how you choose and manage your property, you can look forward to reasonable earnings from hosting on Airbnb. Therefore, choose the location, your room offering, and your target guest audience wisely.

Nowadays, many people rent properties to make some money subletting them on Airbnb, and they are making a tidy sum in the process. This trend has picked up so much that such people have been nicknamed rentpreneurs.

Personal growth

If you have never worked in the hospitality industry, Airbnb offers a window of opportunity into learning skills that will be useful for you at some point in your life. Through Airbnb hosting, you will learn marketing, finance, and customer relations, which are important skills that may be useful in different avenues. You need them in virtually any business venture, and Airbnb offers a good opportunity for you to learn and become better at it.

While interacting with different people from diverse parts of the world, you will also add some creativity into your personal life. There are things you can learn from the guests which, when applied in life, can make a big difference.

Chapter 2: Things to Consider before You Embark on Your Airbnb Journey

The desire to set up your Airbnb and start earning rental income is something most people can appreciate. Perhaps you have a spare bedroom that you can put up for rent and earn from it? Maybe you are stepping up and venturing into Airbnb as a professional with many of properties to manage. With all these are entry points into the business, you can earn a lot.

Before you start dreaming up your empire, there are a few things that you need to think about to guide you to success.

Managing expectations

You want to earn a lot of money from Airbnb. However, what are your goals? You need to think this through so that you know what you are working toward and when you have achieved it. Once you achieve your goals, you should think of something else and build on that.

Some of the ideas that you can think about include creating a secondary income stream, quitting your normal job for a better income through Airbnb, or building a rental business. Whichever goals you have, you must align them with your capital, risk exposure, and the amount of time you have on your hands.

It will take a while before you get a consistent money stream, so disregard posts that you have read online about people making an instant impact on the market. Some of these are not true, while others are out of sheer luck. The truth is, it may take a while before you get a booking and even longer before you get awesome reviews.

Keep your expectations in check, and you will not find yourself stressed when things are taking time to pick up the pace. Most people start small and have to do most of the work on their own, and this includes things like cleaning the premise before a guest checks in and maintaining the lawn. You may be surprised by how much time you need to spend on this, and it can be overwhelming.

As you grow into the business, however, you will learn how to use automation tools for efficiency and save energy and time without affecting the quality of services that you are offering. You may even want to consider bringing in a professional company to manage things like cleaning and maintenance.

Dealing with strangers

As an Airbnb host, you will be dealing with strangers all the time. If you are listing a spare room in your home, you must be ready to invite them to your home. How comfortable are you living with strangers in your home? If this does not work for you, perhaps you need to rethink your strategy, and you may be better off with a separate listing where you do not share the same roof.

Remember that when you are sharing a property with guests, the interaction you have with them will be a part of your reviews, and if you are not welcoming and accommodating, this can lead to negative ones. If you cannot stand the idea of sharing your home with strangers, your best way into the Airbnb venture is to dedicate a separate rental unit to your business.

At the same time, it is not just about interacting or living with strangers, but also about communicating with them and accommodating them, even if they are living in a different property from the one you reside in.

Time constraints

To manage and succeed in your Airbnb venture, you need to set aside sufficient resources, and it may take more time and effort than you expected. Most people go into the Airbnb business without thinking about their strategies. Before you realize it, you cannot afford the time needed to keep things running, and you start slacking.

You should make sure you are available in case of an emergency or if the guest needs clarification about something. Also, ensure your schedule is flexible when your house is booked to cater to the needs of your guests. You can also delegate some duties to someone in case you are unavailable, and communicate this with the guest in good time so they know whom to run to whenever they need assistance.

Unique listing

There are many homes listed on Airbnb—what makes you think yours is special or stands out from the rest? This is a value proposition approach that can help you think about your home from the perspective of a guest.

Why should they look at your property and book it instead of the other properties that are equally good, if not better and perhaps cheaper? Competition is stiff on Airbnb, so you must make sure that you set your property on the right path.

Think about the descriptions and anything else that you will use to showcase your property, and ensure to do a good job at this. Monitor the market to ensure you adjust the property accordingly as competition and the market evolves.

Rapport with the landlords

If like most entrepreneurs on Airbnb, you do not own the home you are listing, it is important to maintain a good relationship with your landlord. A lot of people have listed their properties on Airbnb without their landlord's knowledge, and this goes against so many rules.

First, if anything were to happen to the house during the time a guest was there, you will not be covered by the landlord's homeowners' insurance. The insurer will not take responsibility for claims against the house.

You may have a very good rating on Airbnb and a listing that gets some good reviews and attention, but a bad relationship with your landlord can very quickly damage your reputation. If you plan on subletting the space in your home, talk to your landlord about it, and in good faith, show them that you plan on maintaining a good relationship with them, and you promise to take good care of their property.

Interacting with neighbors

You may have neighbors around your home whether you are leasing it from your landlord or letting your own property. Think about the experience of your neighbors for a moment— how do you think they would feel if they learned that you have been hosting your property on Airbnb? How does this affect the nature of their contract with the landlord or the relevant authorities to which you both subscribe?

In some cities, residents have been petitioning to their respective councils to restrict the use of Airbnb in the premises they reside in, because of disturbances, and in a quiet and small neighborhood, having new faces around every once in a while can create very bad attention.

Liability and risk exposure

Other than your personal safety, when you list your property on Airbnb, you are also exposing yourself to many other risks. There is the risk of theft, damages, and many other concerns. What about your guests? What if they are injured by something in your home that should have been fixed but that you have neglected or kept stalling until it got out of hand? Luckily, Airbnb offers a liability insurance cover that helps you mitigate these risks.

Setting the prices

If you plan on setting one price and sticking to it, you will not be successful on Airbnb. You need to keep monitoring and comparing rates for similar properties to ensure that your pricing strategy is competitive. Monitor special events so that you keep things optimized accordingly and attract more guests. Also, some experts on Airbnb these days use pricing partners to help them get the best rates for their properties.

Adapting to the environment

In any business environment, you must be ready to adapt and change as the market evolves. The same applies to Airbnb. You should monitor the market, read the news, and stay informed about the latest events.

Local legislation changes from time to time, and failure to comply could lead to hefty fines. Also, you have to learn how to position your home to attract different types of travelers at different times of the year.

Necessary interruption

Once you list your home on Airbnb, you must be ready to deal with interruptions. If you are hosting the properties on your own, you need spare time for proper management. If you cannot do that, hire a third-party company to manage and host the properties on your behalf.

As a property manager, you must schedule cleaning, maintenance, and the restocking of supplies that run out. You also need to address complaints from your neighbors and respond to questions from the guests.

For someone who is starting out by amassing properties to build a portfolio, you have to be aware of the disruption and distortion that Airbnb will bring to your life. You may take more time away from the family when starting out, trying to make sure that things are running smoothly. Discuss this with your family so that they are ready for what lies ahead.

Study and understand rental arbitrage

You are getting into a market that is extremely diverse and dynamic, so it is important that you study it and understand it properly before you set out to invest your money in it. Rental markets are not always the same. There will be differences in each market that you can identify, especially when you are listing many properties in diverse areas. Learn how to assess a market in a short time to determine whether you have what it takes to thrive in it or if you need to pass it up for another opportunity.

What are your goals?

Each host has different goals, and outlining them will allow you to easily understand what you are working toward. Some people are interested in earning some money on the side in lieu of the space they have, while others are interested in earning a stable source of income.

With your goals mapped out, you can think about the work needed to get you there, including the planning, capital, and risks that you have to take. Your goals also determine things like the size of your home, the type of listings, strategies, tools that you may need, and the location of your listing.

Understand the market

It is not wise to quit your current job for a new job without knowing the prospects you may face, as you may end up losing something permanent and stable just to be temporarily satisfied.

Most amateur hosts on Airbnb make the mistake of hosting before they know what they are doing and what is out there for them. Airbnb has grown over the years, though there are markets that still do not have the numbers or the demand to sustain hosting. If you are in such a market, it would be insane for you to dive in headfirst.

Study and research the market that you are planning on investing in. If it is a hot market, you can plan around that. If you do not research well, you may end up making less money than what you are supposed to be earning from your effort.

Insurance cover

If you plan on renting your own home, the home insurance plan you have will not cover your home in the event of any damages to the property while you are hosting your house on Airbnb. Once they see the $1 million guarantee that Airbnb offers hosts, most people do not think about this.

Your home is insured as a residential building, not a business premise. Therefore, if anything happens, your insurers will not honor any claim, and you may end up facing losses that can hurt you financially.

Business positioning

As beautiful as your home is, not everyone will be wanting to book it, so you need to ensure you position your listings in a location that appeals to your guests. Say you have business travelers, for example. Such guests would appreciate staying in a place that is close to the business district and will be willing to pay higher rates for the premises.

Chapter 3: Rental Arbitrage—How to Profit without Owning Any Property

The business of rental arbitrage has experienced a boom in recent years, especially as many people realize the potential of doing it through Airbnb. Arbitrage is about looking for disparities in a market and making a profit from price differences. Each market has inefficiencies and imbalances, which you can exploit and earn a tidy sum from.

Through Airbnb, a lot of smart entrepreneurs have been making a lot of money each month, and all this without owning any of the homes. They simply identify some of the inefficiencies in the property market and exploit them. Anyone can do this; as long as you have time and in-depth research skills, you can find properties in the online real estate market and start your business.

One of the benefits that Airbnb has over most of the platforms that offer the same home letting services is the versatility. Since its inception, Airbnb has grown in leaps and bounds, and today, there are many ways through which you can earn from it. Rental arbitrage is one of the methods that have been exploited over the years by witty entrepreneurs, and it has proven to be quite a profitable venture.

In the context of Airbnb, rental arbitrage is the process where you obtain properties and rent them on Airbnb. These properties do not necessarily have to be yours. The idea is to find properties that you can lease for more than what it costs you to obtain it from the owner.

Many people are currently looking for short-term accommodation for one reason or another. Most people would usually opt for a hotel stay, but since people are looking for a "home away from home" kind of setting, a short-term lease on Airbnb makes more sense. There are many restrictions, terms, and conditions that make a hotel stay unfavorable for most people, hence the preference of Airbnb. In an Airbnb setting, you have an entire home to yourself or whatever kind of arrangement that you fancy, without worrying about the normal constraints that are associated with big hotels, especially the cost and convenience.

In most major cities, hotels are extremely pricey. This is true for cities that have lots of tourist attractions or are popular travel destinations. For such markets, Airbnb offers a more affordable alternative for accommodation, which makes a big difference, especially for someone who is planning their trip on a budget.

Through Airbnb arbitrage, you can lease properties in an area that has high demand and charge a higher rate than what the normal property expenses would be. This is true if you can price the unit at a rate that is profitable but still lower than what the hotels are charging in the area.

How to go about rental arbitrage on Airbnb

You must take time and properly research to find the right properties. Study the markets and learn about the peak seasons, the average lease contract terms and values, and what it costs to stay in a hotel. There are many websites where properties are listed either on sale or for lease. Look for properties that have been in the market for a while but that do not seem to be getting any attention. Many times, their owners will be keen to listen to someone who can earn them something from the property.

Once you have selected the ideal property, talk to the owner. You need to convince them that you have the experience and expertise and can make their property earn them money instead of staying listed and not earning anything. Do not just convince the owner, make sure you can actually do what you are promising. This sentiment should be backed up by some research so that you can immediately list the property online, and you can keep your word.

Inform the owner of your plan. These are investments, and at times, they hold more than just monetary value to the owners, so you must be very careful in your approach. They need to see real value addition in allowing you to sublet their property as opposed to having the property sitting pretty in the real estate market and not earning anything.

Remember that if you do not pitch your services well, some landlords will see no sense in giving you the property and would be better off leaving the property lying fallow in the real estate market.

You are pitching a revenue-generating idea to the landlord. Therefore, with this in mind, show them that there is real potential in their property and that you can earn them additional revenue each month from Airbnb. You may have to sweeten the deal for the landlord and perhaps offer to pay them a higher rate than what they are expecting from the property each month. However, do this only if you are certain you have the numbers to back that proposal.

What if the landlord says no?

Well, it is always possible that at first, the landlord objects to your proposal. They may have reservations, which is quite common. However, this should not deter you. It is a chance for you to explain to the landlord your position and how this will be a good proposal for them.

Many times, the landlords are worried about the insurance coverage that they have taken on their properties. The house is insured as a residential facility, not a business premise. Therefore, if anything were to happen to the property, insurers would gladly walk away without honoring any claims, given that the house was not being used for what it was insured for.

This is a valid concern. However, you can explain to the landlord how Airbnb insurance works for their homes. Airbnb offers additional insurance over and above what the normal homeowners' insurance cover offers, with a cover of up to $1 million. This should get the landlord's attention.

When possible, offer a good security deposit on the property so that they can see you are serious about this proposal. One thing that any landlord will be keen on is to see you as someone who is confident and knows what they are doing. It can inspire them, make them believe in you, and be confident that your plan will work for them too.

How much will it cost?

Talking to the landlord may be the easy part. Then, you must also focus on the financials. You are getting an empty house, and it must be furnished tastefully. You need it to be comfortable and convenient for anyone who will want to obtain a lease agreement on Airbnb.

Some of the things that you will need to spend on other than the security deposit include furniture, fixtures, and appliances. Once the landlord agrees to let you use their house, you should bring in furniture and appliances that will make the house as comfortable as possible for your guests. You can refer to the section on important gadgets that you need to have in the Airbnb to see some of the things you need to buy.

Once you have the landlord's permission, the cost of setting up an Airbnb listing will vary. For example, it will cost you more to set up a property in an affluent area. Also, you have to furnish the house according to the environment and neighborhood it is in.

Airbnb projections for rental arbitrage

Your profit targets depend on what your business goals are. However, it is possible for you to know how much you can expect to earn on average from the property beforehand. First, you must know what the average rental rates are for your property. You can research Airbnb for this information. Look at the weekday rates and the weekend rates. Also, compare the rates on holidays. List this information in a spreadsheet so that you can easily compare later on.

Determine how much your expenditure will be. Sum up all your monthly costs and divide this by thirty to get the average daily expenditure rate for your running expenses.

The plan is to make sure that you can turn a profit from the property in less than one month. If it takes longer, you may be too stretched to live up to the expectations you may have set out to the landlord. To be safe, your Airbnb listing should break even each month.

Risks involved in Airbnb arbitrage

While the prospect of earning constant income from properties that you do not own sounds good, there are risks that you need to be aware of. This is an important part of planning because you become aware of what lies ahead. The following are some of the things you need to be on the lookout for:

Regulations

Each jurisdiction has specific regulations that must be adhered to. Therefore, you should research and be aware of the local requirements for the city. There may also be a homeowners' association in the neighborhood where your property is located. Some of the associations may have terms in place that make it difficult for you to get the property on a short-term lease, which means your Airbnb business will be in contravention to their set terms, even if the landlord agrees to lease the property to you. The regulations can hurt your business prospect, especially if you ignore them, because you may be evicted or, worse, risk losing your investment altogether.

Market conditions

In any market, there are forces that determine the increase and decrease in prices, among other things. You must brace yourself for the fact that market conditions are never static, and things can change overnight. Therefore, the demand for property in your selected residential area can also change from one month to the other without notice, so you should have a plan in place to cushion yourself from drastic changes in the market.

Expect the unexpected

Investing in any business is always a risk. There are unseen forces that you must account for. This gives you room for proper planning, especially when you are not renting the property for a few weeks or months.

For example, what happens if your residential area suffers a natural calamity? Do some research on the risk profile for that area to help you determine what your minimum profit will be in the worst-case scenario.

Chapter 4: Getting Permission from Landlords

How do you get a landlord to lease their house to you for your Airbnb business? This is a question that most people have. There are many concerns for both the landlord and yourself, so it is the way you approach the landlord that may make all the difference. Without the landlord's permission, your Airbnb business cannot take off. Some people go behind the landlord's back and list their homes on Airbnb, but this is never a good idea because when things go south, the risk gets higher.

Engaging your landlord before you list their property on Airbnb is about trust and respect. You must establish a rapport with them before they allow you to list the house. Imagine yourself in their shoes for a moment. Would you be comfortable with the same request? Think about the pros and cons like a property owner. What kind of tenants would you hope to get? This may seem like a simple discussion, but what is at stake for the landlord is so much more than that.

Before you engage your landlord, you must make sure you have valid reasons that will make them see value in your discussion. At the same time, make sure you are not pitching like a salesperson. Have some respect in your approach. Most people have invested a lot of time, money, and relationships to get the properties they have, so renting them to a third party may be a tricky venture.

It is obvious that the majority of landlords will balk at the idea of listing their property on Airbnb, and this also explains why a lot of properties on Airbnb are leased without the consent of the landlords—which is a very bad idea. Why is that so? If you get caught, you will be evicted, and you may also lose all your earnings. Should the landlord take legal action against you, you can lose so much more.

Approach the landlord as you would any other person. Talk to them. Perhaps they are willing to do it, but you never asked. A landlord will appreciate the fact that you approached them with the idea of listing the house on Airbnb instead of going behind their backs. This is a brilliant way of establishing goodwill.

Understand your landlord

You have a higher chance of negotiating a deal with your landlord if you understand their position. Whether the landlord has one property or many, consider some of the factors that influence their decision making.

Look at it this way; for most landlords, their properties are a source of income with low risk, hence long-term investments. You will realize that most lease contracts expire in less than three years.

Some landlords earn quite a fortune from their properties, while others use rent as a side hustle. Whatever the case, most landlords consider earning rental income as a low-risk venture for the long haul.

Logically, landlords do not find it reasonable to spend resources on their properties, as these should be income streams for the future. Therefore, once a tenant has moved in, they tend to shy away from spending on the properties. Two of their worst fears are having a tenant who damages their property or losing a good tenant. These can be mitigated by replacing the tenant, however long it will take, or by getting a good home insurance cover.

Now, picture a situation where your tenant tells you that they want to sublet your property to random strangers from time to time, all while making profit. This idea alone is a high risk for any landlord.

Risks involved

There are many reasons once the Airbnb discussion is on the table, the once-low-risk investment becomes a high-risk investment for the landlord. On their part, Airbnb will verify the guests who visit homes listed on their profile. However, there are always a few sour grapes that find their way through and damage property, steal, or harass neighbors.

There are also jurisdictions where short-term leases are not allowed, and you can be fined if found in contravention of the regulations. More importantly, however, any landlord is supposed to have homeowners' insurance for their property.

To mitigate any risks to the property, ensure you communicate with your landlord and Airbnb in good time. Claims arise all the time, and Airbnb has a time limit for responding to claims. Any damaged items in the house can only be replaced or repaired if you have original receipts.

Given these concerns, it is understandable that most landlords will not see the point of leasing the space for Airbnb. For this reason, most of the landlords will only allow you to lease their property on Airbnb if they are getting something in return.

Speaking to your landlord

One of the first mistakes that you may make is to approach the landlord with a business proposal. Most people are attached to their investments, and the same applies to landlords. This is a personal venture for them. You may not know the sacrifices that they made to be where they are today, and owning the property you are interested in. Therefore, if you approach your landlord with a business proposal without considering their personal sentiments, you will probably fail to get their approval.

What you need to do is address the risks that are involved and offer them a solution that appeals to their needs. In some cases, you will have to increase your rent payments. Landlords want assurance that their property will be in good hands, so offer to take personal responsibility for anything that happens in the house, including repairs and maintenance.

Before you consult your landlord, however, make sure you are ready for what lies ahead. One of the things that will matter is your personal relationship or connection with the landlord. It is easier for you if you have been a good tenant and have a strong relationship with the landlord.

If the space is shared with other tenants, how do you propose to go about it? What will make the difference in the interaction between your guests and the landlord's tenants? Is there any way the presence of your Airbnb guests will affect the landlord's tenants?

If these factors work for you, you can quickly get their approval. Also, keep in mind that you may have to get creative to get a positive response from the landlord. However, be careful not to promise anything that you cannot deliver.

There are some reasonable promises that you can make, including an extension of the lease, offering to pay either more in rent or a percentage of what you earn from Airbnb. Also, you can also offer your rent upfront.

Inform the landlord how the Airbnb insurance guarantee works, and that other than their homeowners' insurance, Airbnb also offers $1 million in insurance protection. The landlord will also appreciate you having more control over the rentals, including limiting the type of people that you can allow into the premise or specific groups of people. This may also depend on the community where the property is listed. Increasing your security deposit with the landlord is another factor that will be useful.

Chapter 5: Market Research—an Important Step to Help Ensure Profitability

If you are involved in any business today, you must learn how to perform market research. This helps you understand your market better, the competition, and any other factors that affect your business operation. The same applies to Airbnb. There are many tools available at your disposal. Lots of people are earning thousands of dollars from managing other people's houses on Airbnb, and it all comes down to efficient market research.

For efficient market research, you will need a few important tools; AirDNA and Airbnb. When used properly, these tools help you determine the appropriate location, something that most people struggle with.

While there is a lot of information that you can get from Airbnb for free, most of it is not extensive enough to help you make a wise investment decision, and you will need to delve deeper into paid tools to get lots of credible information.

AirDNA

For someone who has never used it before, AirDNA can seem

a bit complex. However, it provides data that you would not be able to find anywhere else. This is the type of data that will help you make the leap from a beginner to an expert. You can make informed, intelligent decisions based on this data and thus grow your business.

Why do you need AirDNA?

One of the biggest mistakes that most people make when venturing into the Airbnb business is failing to understand their competition and the market that they operate in. Going about this blindly will cost you, and could end up ruining any hopes you had of making it.

There are two types of hosts in the Airbnb business. Either you are a prospective host, or you are an existing host who has been letting homes for a long time. If you are hoping to start hosting, you need to know what the prospects are. For an existing host, the data you get on AirDNA will help you determine where you are lagging behind, streamline your business, and improve your overall performance.

For many beginner hosts, the desire to earn money from Airbnb comes from stories that they hear about people who have made it and are earning lots of money online. Immediately, you imagine yourself turning your free time into an empire. You rush into the business unaware of what is involved, and before you know it, you fail and are miserable, yet people around you seem to be doing just fine with their homes on Airbnb.

There is a lot of growth in Airbnb as a whole, and the company keeps advancing and coming up with innovative updates for the services that they offer on their platform. What is your stake in this growth? As Airbnb expands into new territories and markets, new opportunities come up. Using AirDNA will help you better understand these metrics, and map a plan of action before you delve into letting homes as a business.

The AirDNA Mechanism

For you to get the most out of AirDNA, you must understand how the system works. This helps you understand what it does and how it will be useful to you. All the data and reports that you get on AirDNA are built from reports and data that is collected from the Airbnb website. All this information is available in the public domain, so there is no violation of anyone's privacy involved. There are millions of listings on Airbnb, and they are all tracked by the AirDNA database. From here, the reports are updated and used to support the Market Minder, an innovative tool in AirDNA.

While there are several tools out there that can help you in machine learning and AI for the home listing business, AirDNA is probably the best tool you will come across. One of the perks of using AirDNA is that their machine learning and AI capabilities are so enhanced that they can tell the difference between a blocked day and a booked day. This level of accuracy takes away the need for guesswork.

You have a map on the home screen that offers the same functionality you get in Google Maps. You can also see the competition, listed under *Professional Hosts*. This shows you how many people have more than one listing that is currently active and this can help you figure out what your competition looks like.

From the home screen, you can easily determine the nature of the market. Markets are graded accordingly and assigned ratings depending on the location. You can also see the regulations, seasonal consideration, demand for rent, and the rental activity in the selected area. The following are some things you need to keep in mind:

- A low-regulation score means there is a high level of regulation in the area.

- A high-revenue growth score indicates an increase in revenue for each listing.

- A high-rental demand score means there is a high demand for the properties.

- A high-seasonality score indicates a very low change between the low and high seasons.

What you can do is record this data in an Excel sheet, and you can use this as a point of reference in the future for a number of cities you are interested in.

Pricing strategy

AirDNA also gives a pricing breakdown that makes it easier for you to analyze and make predictions. The prices are grouped into the following:

- Average daily rate (ADR)

- The ADR range

- Available rates and future supply

You can view the active rentals in a graph or calendar view. You can also get information about the total number of properties that have been booked.

Some other useful information that you will find is the occupancy rate. The booking lead time in this section indicates how long it takes (in days) before someone makes a booking.

The seasonality and revenue feature allows you to narrow down statistics to the date of the month. You can easily see the best month for business, from where you can decide how you want to price your rates to maximize your earnings.

AirDNA also has an amenities feature that allows you to see what other listings have in their facilities. This is a good way to determine what makes your competitors better than you are, and you can use this information to figure out how to catch up or beat them.

Identifying the competition

Airbnb is growing at an unprecedented rate, with more than three thousand listings being added on the platform every day. This has made Airbnb one of the go-to solutions for a lot of people who are looking for a place to stay, as opposed to using hotels.

Booking your stay in an Airbnb property is easy. Locations to homes are provided clearly, and guests have a lot of convenient support tools at their disposal, especially if they do not like what they see.

With more properties being listed on the platform, you will want to get the best rates for your listings. The more properties are added, the higher the chances that prices will be lower since users have access to a wide pool of options. As a host, you should look into ways to understand and beat the competition.

You cannot fight what you cannot see. Therefore, you need to know the nature of the competition. You will know what the market looks like, the neighborhoods, the rates, and the supply of quality homes.

For a beginner, especially if you do not have reviews yet, set your rates lower than most of the competition. If you set your rates low enough, you should get some inquiries on the property. A few reviews down the line, you can increase your rate to match the market rates.

You can use services like Everbooked or AirDNA to help you set the right price for your listing. These services analyze the competitors and help you set a dynamic price for your property. Even with all the tools available at your disposal, you still need to research well to find out the listings that are active in your neighborhood. Luckily, Airbnb has an innovative search function that makes all this work easy for you. You can find out the descriptions, headlines, photos, and prices for the listings in a region you are interested in.

In the search filter, you can determine the most popular places in the neighborhood, those that are relevant to your listing, and so on. Save the URL with the filtered settings so that you can always refer to it from time to time to see if any changes are relevant to your listing which match your requirements.

Factors that affect your listing

Even as you are working to define and beat the competition, you should realize that sometimes, you could be your own undoing. You can have as much information about the competition as possible, but without understanding what to do with it, your efforts will be futile.

Several factors determine the way listings will appear in search results when someone wants to book a home. Airbnb is designed in a way to make it as easy as possible for guests so that they can find a suitable home in as short a time as possible for their trip. The first thing you should do, therefore, even before you look at your competitors, is to know what the guests are after.

Three important things determine how your listing will look in search results. These are the following:

Trip details

This concerns everything about the trip, like how long it will take, the number of people who are on the trip, when the trip is due, and so on. Does the guest have a set maximum price that they are looking for?

Listing details

Regarding your listing, what matters is the reviews, location, and price. Do you have an instant booking on your listing? How fast do you respond to issues and requests that are raised?

Guest preferences

Airbnb considers a lot of features unique to the guest to help in listing your home. Some of these factors include where the guest is searching from, any previous trips they have had, or if they have homes in their wish lists. This can influence the ranking for your home.

The psychology of a guest is an important consideration. What do they think about when looking for a home to stay for a few days? This determines how your listing will perform in an Airbnb search. Airbnb will consider whether guests often make a booking when they see your listing. More often, a successful listing will help guests easily book their holiday. A successful listing is also one that gets clicks when it shows up in search results. This is because guests are eager to find out more about that listing.

As a host, since Airbnb is a free market, there are things that you do not have control over, but influence the ranking of your home. That being said, however, there are other factors that you can control about your listing. These include the following:

Price

This is one of the most important things that guests look at, especially when they are comparing different listings. Therefore, you need to research well and settle on a price that is fair and competitive in the market you are listing it in.

Are you a Superhost?

The fact that you are a Superhost will not necessarily boost your listing. However, there are factors that move you from a normal host to a Superhost, and these factors will definitely help you improve the ranking of your listing.

Reviews

In the hospitality industry, reviews are an important tool that you cannot take for granted. The rankings for homes as they appear in searches consider the number of trips and reviews that are left by guests about your home. You should always strive to get good reviews. However, a few negative ratings will not have a big impact on your overall rating.

Helping new listings

If you have a new listing, you may worry about competing

against well-established listings on Airbnb. However, you should not be bothered by this, as Airbnb makes sure that new hosts get their properties listed and established and show up in search rankings.

User experience

Even as you are running your business on Airbnb, remember that the ultimate goal for Airbnb is to make sure that people can keep coming to the platform whenever they need a holiday. Airbnb strives for a positive experience for everyone. Because of this, hosts and listings that have proven to be very responsive are often elevated. If, for example, you can respond to queries in less than twenty-four hours, this will boost your ranking online.

A lot of guests appreciate a seamless and fast-booking experience. Therefore, if you have *Instant Booking* enabled on your listing, there is a good chance that people will be more likely to book your home, as the Airbnb algorithm automatically boosts listings that have enabled this feature. This should not deter you, however, because even if you have a *Request to Book* instead of an Instant Booking, but the listing is doing well based on other factors that determine the guest experience, it will still perform well in the search rankings.

If you choose to have a Request to Book on your listing, the search ranking will track the number of guests who are denied a booking, even after requesting to book. While it is common to reject a Request to Book, there are other factors at play which will determine if this affects your rating and the appearance of your listing in search results.

As you build and update your listing, you must pay attention to important details that attract guests. For example, research phrases and words that you can use in your description and titles. There is a lot of room for growth in Airbnb as more features are added, and as a host, there is so much that you can do to benefit from this.

Visibility

It takes six to twenty-four hours for your property to become visible once you have listed it on the platform. This is to allow you sufficient time to check your settings and make sure you are comfortable with things as they are.

Some guests prefer to take a listing for a long-term stay. For such guests, you must indicate whether your listing allows this. You can also offer a discount for such long-term stays for it to be more appealing to guests.

The Airbnb system is constantly being upgraded to provide guests and hosts the best possible platform. Try to stay informed and abreast with the latest information, especially since some features and factors are often tested, adjusted, and upgraded accordingly.

Chapter 6: Furnishing Your Airbnb

Furnishing the Airbnb rental is just as important as finding the right location. You need to make sure that your guests are all happy, satisfied, and comfortable. You have to choose the right furniture for the house. When choosing furniture, you must make sure you get two things right, form and function. Which pieces of furniture do you think are perfect for the guests? Are they satisfactory? Spare enough time to research and shop for furniture so that you spend within your budget and get the selection process right.

Functionality

Think about the role that the furniture will play and the challenges that it will help you overcome.

Fulfilling the needs of your guests is important to make sure that they have a seamless, awesome experience when they stay in your home. In this stance, you are targeting a specific audience. Assuming you are looking for business travelers who will be hosted in a studio apartment, you must make sure you furnish the apartment in a manner that will be suitable for them. This means you must have a desk where they can work and a comfortable bed.

The setting should ooze productivity, making it an easy place for accommodation for people who are working hard. Spend your money furnishing it in a way that your guests will not just feel comfortable but will also appreciate the utility value. They need to feel like you had them in mind when selecting your furniture.

Even if you decide to go all modern with the furnishing, try not to complicate things. Do not invest in furniture that may be difficult for the user to work with. At times, something as simple as that can ruin your guest's trip.

Furniture form

The furniture's form is about its appeal. What furniture are you looking for, and what will it look like? You do not want to have an eyesore in the house, in the name of something fashionable. The other challenge that most hosts will struggle with when looking at form is the budgetary allocation. You may have to spend a bit more on a unique piece of furniture, but in the long run, it may be the one thing that gets you more bookings, so it will be a worthy purchase.

The type of furniture you have in the house can also determine the price you set for the listing. In case you have average furniture in the listing photos, you may not be able to charge high rates for the premise. Besides, everyone will decide on whether to live in your home or not based on the photos that they see online. Therefore, make sure that your furniture and photos can properly sell your home to the guests.

Is your home in a place that experiences huge user traffic? If this is the case, think about the type of furniture in terms of duration. If you expect lots of bookings, look for furniture that is heavy duty as compared to most furniture items. These items will be used often, so they should be able to stand the test. No one likes to go on a furniture purchase run more than once in a very short time.

Whenever you are shopping for furniture, think about the stability of the furniture. Ask yourself whether it can very easily break. Try to look for furniture that takes a lot of effort to break.

As a rule of thumb, glass-top tables should be avoided at all costs. They may look neat and appealing, but there is always a risk of the glass breaking. When the glass top breaks, you will have to think about replacing it. You will also have to worry about the damages and whether the guest will pay for them or not. You must also think about injuries that can occur. This raises a potential for conflict because the damages may happen because of an accident that is not of the guest's doing, but you cannot agree with them.

Before a new guest arrives, your house needs to be thoroughly cleaned. It is not the best idea to have furniture that takes a long time to clean. The longer it takes to clean it, the more money it will cost. You also need to realize that some items simply should not feature in the house. Take the example of an accent light made of a thousand crystal pieces. It is beautiful, but it is not necessary for your Airbnb. Anything that has many crevices should be avoided, because the crevices hold a lot of dust, and it will take you a very long time to clean it.

Planning

According to statistical information on Airbnb, most of the planned stays are usually done by ladies. It may be a mother, girlfriend, a wife, and so forth. Therefore, you must ensure you furnish the house in such a way that can appeal to the things they want to see when they go on holiday.

When planning your furniture purchases, consider going after the deals that are offered by furniture stores, as this is a great way to save some money in the process. Research and ask about the interest offers, then plan around that.

As you plan to furnish your home, there are four things that you must think about: simplicity, cleanliness, toughness, and charm. These are important in determining what ambiance your property will give off when someone walks in.

People like to take photos of something cool that they come across, especially in an Airbnb, and they will probably post it on Instagram. Make sure that you have at least one item that will get the attention of your host, and put it in a focal point in the house. Given that this item will be getting lots of attention and photos, it must be durable to stand all the pressure.

In case you are still unsure of what to do in regards to furnishing your home, it is a good idea to get inspired by the top hosts in your region. You can look at what they have done in their houses or use that as a guideline to help you make your home look awesome. Instagram and Pinterest are two other places where you can find inspiration to furnish your home in a simple yet elegant way.

Decorating guide for your Airbnb

Decoration and making sure the rental property is worth the attention you need it to get can be quite intimidating. In case you do not have experience in interior design and decoration, you may find this to be a daunting process. We will discuss some ideas that will help you make sure you get the decoration right and make your home one of the best places anyone who visits can spend time in.

The first rule of decoration is to make sure you do not break your bank. You must find the right balance between what you are willing to spend and how to get things right. Here are some useful tips that will help you make sure you get nothing but the best result when decorating your home:

Identify the target audience

What type of guests are you looking forward to having in your home? Think about the guest profile, and it will be easier for you to settle on the type of decorations that you need. The decorations for budget travelers, weekend getaway visitors, business guests, and families are not always the same.

You should try and understand what each of these categories of guests needs and offer it. Try and make your home one of the most irresistible places they have ever visited and in the future, you will get more repeat bookings and referrals.

The better you understand the guests, the easier it will be for you to know what they want and how to respond to their needs. You can also use the interaction and exchanges to learn about the new trends and things that the specific type of traveler appreciates in an Airbnb home.

Take the case of a home by the beach—you would need to invest in some beach chairs and toys, especially if you are listing it for families on vacation. If you are targeting business audiences, you must make sure you have a printer and a workspace.

In some cases, a laptop would also come in handy for people who travel light and have their documents stored on the cloud. Also, it goes without saying that you need high-speed internet in the house too. Many of the hosts these days even offer free iPhone services to their guests, especially if they are international business travelers.

Decorating your rental

Some simple things such throw pillows may not be considered by most but will go a long way in determining how comfortable your home setting is. Go out of your way to create the right ambiance for your guests. You will get amazing reviews, and these will further translate into additional bookings.

After well decorating your home, invest in a good photographer. You can do this on your own or get an expert to take photos of the house. Try not to use too many filters as these can make your home look fake.

Guests often complain about homes that are made to look

glamorous in online photos while they're actually an eyesore in real-life. Decorate your home well, and be genuine in the photos you post online. Remember that if you try to hoodwink your guests by using photos that present a different picture of your furnishings than what is real, you will be exposed in the reviews, and your listing may be reported to Airbnb for stern action.

Theme selection

Guests on Airbnb are always looking for something unique, something that makes your home stand out from most that they have been to or something that will make their stay in your home a memorable one. No one wants a small hotel room that is squeezed and closeted.

Your role is to ensure you create an authentic place that they can go to and still feel at home when they are so far away from it. Choosing the right theme for your premise may sound like a challenge, but you can use a few things in your vicinity to inspire a confident theme choice.

Say your property is by the beach, for example. You can use beach accessories to bring a beach atmosphere to life. On the other hand, rustic log cabins may be the perfect option for someone whose home is located in a mountainous region. These are the simple things that you can consider which will make a big difference to your home.

Furnishing the home with art can be a tricky affair. Unless you are appealing to an artsy group of travelers, you must be very careful with the way you use art. Something that you consider subtle may be a tad bit too much for the average guest, or they may fail to recognize the importance of the work of art you have in your home.

Useful decoration tips

Contrary to popular belief, decorating your home as a rental may be cheaper and easier than decorating your own home. Think of it as a showroom, and you want to appeal to a lot of people without spending too much in the process. The following are some useful guidelines that you can use to decorate the property tastefully:

Color selection

Always use neutral colors for your walls, and for furnishings, use natural wood. The goal here is to make sure you are appealing to a lot of people without breaking the bank.

Accent pieces

Accent pieces are added for character. Do not pack too many pieces at the same time. Start with something as simple as one painting, a piece of pottery, or a colorful furniture item. You can use this as the focal point, and based on this, select complementing colors for everything else that is in the house.

Context

To establish the context in the house, use different textures, adding an element of unique interest wherever the textures contrast. Careful use of fabrics will also help you in wall hangings, window coverings, slipcovers and throw pillows.

Bed space

You can increase your potential rental income by maximizing the space on your beds. A pull-out couch or a futon in the living room can help you host more people in the same space and earn more. If you have a spare room, you can add two beds inside.

Some hosts put the beds together to support a couple or two children. In the master bedroom, ensure you have the biggest mattress of the lot. For a family home, a baby cot would be a good addition. You can also add an air mattress for convenience.

Spacious setting

You do not want to have the guests banging their bags against your furniture or walls, so make sure you have enough room available. Leave as much space as possible between the rooms and the front door.

Electrical outlets

Make sure you have enough electrical items for a convenient stay. These include phone chargers and extension cords.

Using doormats

Have a doormat outside the door to protect your carpet and floor. If you choose the right doormat, it can also accentuate the home and make it more appealing.

To add warmth to your home, use textiles and rugs. These can create a visual appeal that makes the room look more homely. You can also choose the textiles and rugs carefully to match your lounge chairs or whichever setting you have in the house so that they complement the decor and make the room look great.

Careful mirror placement

Mirrors, when placed in the right place, make your home look more spacious and will also help to improve the lighting situation.

While these are things that you should do to make your home more appealing and comfortable for guests, there are other things you should avoid altogether. For example, get rid of clutter from your home. Things like comic figurines may be your thing, but they may not be appealing to your guests.

Personal items have no place in your Airbnb listing. Do not

include personal toiletries, clothing, family photos, and anything else that may be of personal value to you. Other than the fact that they may not appeal to your guests, they can get damaged in the process, especially with children in the house.

Do you have a political or religious piece somewhere in the house? Remove it before listing the house. Chances are, the guest coming to your home does not share the same beliefs. Besides, the idea is to make sure that your guests are comfortable in the house and not distracted by your thoughts and beliefs. Some people hold strong sentiments about the things they believe in and may check out of your property as soon as they realize you share a differing belief to theirs.

Expensive and antique furniture has no place in an Airbnb setting. You may be excited about creating a comfortable space for your guests, but you do not have to spend this much. These types of furniture are only good for your personal space, not for a business setting. For functionality, use normal furnishings that are tasteful but that do not demand a lot in budgetary outlay.

The living room

Your living room should have a welcome appeal to guests, offering an assurance that they made the perfect choice in booking your property. A big living room that is airy appeals to a lot of people. Choose your furniture carefully, making sure that it is comfortable and that it does not crowd the room.

Choose seats that are proportionate to your home. Make sure

they are neither too bulky nor too weak. To make them cozier, add some cushions. You can also include a convertible couch in the living room for which you can charge extra.

A coffee table is a good addition to your home. However, make sure it is not too fragile, like a glass coffee table. They provide a good setting for snacks and drinks when the guests are having fun indoors.

The bedroom

The bedroom should be set in a way that it gives off a sweet sleeping ambiance. The colors should not be too noisy. It is a room that is designed for comfort, so get a bed that fits at least two people comfortably. If you have additional bedrooms, a smaller bed or a convertible sofa can save you a lot of space.

The lighting in the bedroom should not be too bright. You can use table lamps with warm lighting, as this is a room that someone should go to and easily fall asleep in.

The bedroom and living room are two of the most important rooms in any Airbnb listing. Other than these two, furnish rooms like the kitchen and bathroom tastefully, but within your budget.

Announcing...A <u>HUGE</u> Secret Your Competitors Don't Want You to Know!

Here is **just a fraction** of what you will discover with the FREE bonus:

- 6 Hidden Secrets to Develop a Positive Attitude
- How To Get and **<u>STAY</u>** Motivated
- How To Tap Into Your **<u>Unique</u>** Creative Side To Differentiate Yourself
- How To Become An Efficient Problem Solver

... and **so much more**!

Download your copy of this FREE guide now by clicking on the link below!:

http://bit.ly/SecretsForAirbnb

Chapter 7: Must Have Gadgets for Airbnb Hosts

If you plan on making your Airbnb listing one of the best in the neighborhood, you must think about comfort. These days, there are devices that people need to have around to make them feel comfortable. These devices are mainly used for convenience, but they go a long way in making a guest's stay in your home perfect.

Even though people travel to cities far from where they live, they still want that homely experience. The average hotel room barely has the right gadgets, and this explains why more people are inclined to choosing an Airbnb listing over staying there. The following are some simple gadgets that would make your listing really stand out:

Chargers

Nowadays, everyone needs a charger. Your guests may or may not have carried theirs, so having a set of convenient chargers in your home is a plus. Multiport USB chargers are available online, and they go for as low as ten dollars.

Today, many devices can make your house more comfortable and stylish. A wireless charger, for example, is a great addition to have, as it removes the annoyance of having cables all over the place. Besides, the ability for guests to charge their devices wherever they are in the house is something they will definitely appreciate.

Entertainment

You do not really need a full-scale theater in your home to make it one of the best. However, investing in some quality in-home entertainment will make a big difference. Ensure the house is fitted with some modern entertainment gadgets, like a widescreen TV, subscription to HBO, Netflix, and the like.

Since most guests carry other devices on holiday other than their phones, make sure you have an HDMI cable around or any other peripherals that can help them connect their devices to your TV. Can you afford a projector? If so, having one in the house will be a major plus. You want your guests to enjoy their stay in your home, complete with amazing entertainment.

Media streaming device

Most people, if not everyone, use streaming devices. There are many streaming options available today, like Roku, Apple TV, Amazon, Fire Stick, or Chromecast. Most of these devices can also be used without worrying about them being stolen.

Thermostats

Before your guests arrive, you need to already have the house air-conditioned. This means that you have to make your way to the listing. What happens if you are far away? A smart thermostat would come in handy. You can program it to detect when the house is occupied and adjust the settings accordingly. Disclose this to your guests so that they can also make use of the thermostat to make their living space as comfortable as they need it to be.

Innovative lighting

Energy costs keep rising, and to prevent them from eating into your profits, you should find a way to keep them reasonable. Smart lights are, therefore, for your protection. When the guest checks out, you will know whether the lights remained turned on. For security, you can also set your lights to operate in a way that would indicate someone is in the house, even when the listing is vacant.

Smart speakers

It is understandable that having portable gadgets in the house is a concern for most people, as there is the risk that you go back and find it missing. Back in the day, this would have been a challenge, especially since most of these gadgets would be very expensive to obtain in the first place. Nowadays, however, you can get a portable speaker for as little as twenty dollars.

It is not just about the cost of obtaining these devices, but also about the convenience that comes with owning them. Your guests should be able to enjoy the convenience of speaking to Google Assistant or Alexa and getting recommendations for things like coffee shops, restaurants, or anything else that they normally do when they are at home.

You can also program an assistant like Alexa to provide useful information about the home to your guests, such as the password to your wireless network, or anything else that may be useful to them.

Should you choose to have a smart speaker at home, remember to create a specific account for your listing from your normal account. Guests will appreciate the ability to control devices by voice.

Programmable smart locks

Smart locks are the next level in security. There are several challenges that you would face when using a physical set of keys that you do not have to worry about with smart locks. It is fairly easy to duplicate a physical key, which increases the security risk for the property. Also, the keys can get lost.

Many hosts struggle to control checkout times when using physical keys, and this poses a challenge, especially if there is a very short time between the time a guest checks out and the time another comes in. Also, it becomes a problem when you are not in town.

Smart locks can be programmed in a way that guests have a temporary access code. This code remains active from the moment the guest checks in and expires when their check-out time is due. You can control access from wherever you are. With smart locks, you can also set parameters for whoever has access to the property, such as cleaners and maintenance crews at specific times.

Innovative doorbell

Doorbells have come a long way. You have innovative doorbells that you can use, which will make it easier for you and your guests to have an awesome Airbnb experience. On the part of your guests, a video doorbell, for example, will make it easier for them to know who is outside before they open the door.

For the host, a video doorbell that you can monitor remotely can help you keep track of the number of people who are using your premise, especially if you charge per person, and extra for any additional guests that were not disclosed earlier.

Video doorbells can also help you keep tabs on pets for homes that enforce strict no-pet policies. Many guests tend to ignore these simple rules and may try to sneak in a pet without your permission.

Think about the security and convenience of having a video doorbell. Should one of your guests lose access to their phones or be unable to unlock the door, they can interact with you through the video doorbell, and you would unlock the door for them. For the sake of privacy, any device that can transmit or record still images, audio, or video when they check into your premise needs to be disclosed to your guests beforehand.

Security camera

The first thing about installing a security camera is that you must disclose it to your guests. Today, very few people feel uneasy in the presence of security cameras, especially in the perimeter of the property. This is important for your security as well as theirs. Airbnb advises hosts to ensure the security of their properties and their guests, and one of the ways to do this is by installing these cameras.

Other than listing the presence of security cameras in your property, you also should make sure they are not set in private or sensitive parts of the house, like the bathroom or bedroom.

Motion sensor

You can choose to restrict access to some parts of the property, especially where you keep personal things, like in the basement. Motion sensors can alert you in case your guest wander off into parts of the premise that they are explicitly advised not to enter.

Just as you would with security cameras, you also need to ensure your guest is aware of the presence of motion sensors in the building. Airbnb has strict guidelines to follow for the use of motion sensors.

Airbnb insurance advice

Airbnb hosts enjoy up to a million dollars in liability

coverage, and all this comes without an additional cost. There are two types of protection that Airbnb offers users, host protection insurance and host guarantee.

Host Protection Insurance

A property owner is always concerned about the risk of claims issued against their properties or their person. Some of the common claims that can arise are third-party claims which are raised when someone is injured on the property or in the event of any damage to the property.

In most cases, a homeowner will already have their normal insurance cover to mitigate such circumstances. However, if you are hosting on Airbnb, you would need to consider extending your cover. The normal insurance policy only covers you up to the extent of the terms and conditions of your engagement. An Airbnb listing is a rental contract, and for this reason, you need additional cover for the property as a rental listing, and for the risk of damage or injury to and by the guests on the property.

Airbnb offers insurance cover in more than twelve countries, with liability protection not exceeding $1 million. These covers are only applicable in case a claim is made during the course of a guest's stay in your property.

What if you already have another insurance cover for your property? Would there be a clash with the Airbnb cover? No. It is wise to have both because the Airbnb insurance cover protects you in the course of your Airbnb business. A normal homeowner insurance policy will only cover your property under the terms of the agreement that you signed when you entered into the contract. Should something happen to your guest, the Airbnb insurance will cover any of the qualifying costs, which takes away the challenges that you would encounter if you relied only on your local insurance provider.

As a host on Airbnb, you are automatically covered under the Airbnb Host Protection Insurance program. You may not know it, but each time you put up a home for rent, you agree to a contract protecting your property.

Liability under the Airbnb insurance cover

It is wise to know what is covered under the Airbnb insurance policy. The Airbnb insurance cover is no different from any other insurance policy that you may take. There is a limit to the responsibility Airbnb takes for damages. The following are some of the damages that the insurance coverage does not cover:

- Molestation or sexual abuse by the guest, host, or any other party
- Bacteria or fungi in the premise
- Battery and assault
- Loss of earnings
- Communicable diseases
- Terrorism-related activities
- Advertising injury

- Personal injuries
- Silica, lead, or asbestos
- Pollution

Difference between Airbnb host guarantee and Airbnb host protection insurance

You should be aware that the host guarantee on Airbnb is not insurance but, rather, a feature that Airbnb offers homeowners to help protect their property from damages that may happen to their homes during a guest's stay. Besides, as a host, in special circumstances, you can ask for a security deposit from guests. The additional liability cover that you get from Airbnb is to cover any concern you may have as a homeowner before you lease out your property, especially if you are afraid that the listing may affect your normal home insurance.

While the Airbnb host guarantee is a brilliant feature that will protect you, it does not offer blanket protection. The Airbnb host guarantee does not cover personal liability, pets or cash and any securities you may have in the premise. To be safe, before listing your property on Airbnb, make sure you have homeowner's insurance. You should also take precautionary measures when renting out property. Remove any valuable items that you may have in your home and store them in a safe space.

Airbnb cleaning fees

A clean house will keep your guests happy, satisfied, and repeatedly coming back to your home. However, cleaning is one of the things that most hosts are afraid of. Imagine spending hours on end cleaning up before and after your guests arrive. Some guests may leave your home much dirtier than most, especially when they have children around, or if they had a party, for example.

Do you have enough time to dedicate to cleaning? If not, you must plan to get a cleaning service. This explains why Airbnb listings have a cleaning fee. The question is, how much should you charge, and how do you arrive at the said figure?

Airbnb charges guests a one-time cleaning fee for the cleaning that is done by the host or cleaning service before the guest's arrival. Some hosts choose not to charge the cleaning fee but may include it in their hosting fee without explicitly mentioning it. The following is a brief guide that will let you know how to set the right cleaning fee.

Property size

You must apportion your cleaning rates depending on the size of your listing. You cannot charge the same cleaning fee for a studio apartment as someone who is leasing out a four-bedroom mansion. Therefore, you have to be realistic when setting your cleaning fees. Consult widely. You can even ask a professional cleaning service to visit your home and give you a cleaning quote, then use this to guide your cost.

When you are renting out a private room in your home, it gets trickier. You already have the rest of the house on a cleaning schedule, apart from the one room that you are leasing out. Think about the time you will need to clean the room and plan accordingly.

Type of property

Think about the property you are listing for a moment. Are you listing it as a luxury property? How would you describe the neighborhood it is located in? In case you have luxurious property, you may be inclined to charge a higher fee for cleaning than a listing in a regular place.

Study the competition

Another way to learn how much you can charge for cleaning is to see what other hosts are charging in your area. Look at properties of a similar size to yours. If they are charging seventy dollars on average for cleaning, it is wise for you to do the same, especially if your properties are similar in size as well as amenities.

Guest expectations

Some hosts have special cleaning instructions for their hosts. For example, some hosts request their guests to clean up before they leave. This involves things like doing the dishes or stripping the bed.

Other than that, if your cleaning rate is too low, some guests who have experience with Airbnb may feel that they may need to do some cleaning of their own. It is wise to clarify any special cleaning instructions for your guests beforehand so that they know what they are signing up for and neither of you ends up frustrated.

Remember that most guests will treat your home based on the instructions that you set. If you set a high cleaning cost, guests will probably not want to do simple things like cleaning up because they expect you to have someone or a system in place for that. If you do not, they will feel cheated.

Hiring experts

Another option will be to get a professional team to handle cleaning services for you. This is good if you have many properties or if, for some reason, you are unable to do the cleaning on your own. Ensure that you select an expert cleaning crew. Go over their terms and conditions to know what you are paying for, then factor this into your cleaning rate when listing your property on Airbnb.

Trial and error

Another way of setting the cost of cleaning is to try playing around with the rates. In case you are getting a lot of bookings at the price that you have set, think about increasing it a little, and see if this affects your earnings. The idea here is to ensure you are getting the maximum profit from the property.

However, stay reasonable. If you are charging around one hundred dollars for cleaning, for example, guests would expect to be staying for at least a week. Unless you are listing a luxury property, charging someone one hundred dollars for cleaning for a day's hosting is unreasonable.

Chapter 8: Listing Wizardry

Writing powerful descriptions

While you can tell so much about a property by the pictures, the description is just as important. Descriptions answer a lot of questions that may not be answered in the pictures. Your guests are looking for thorough and precise descriptions.

You have to make sure you provide an accurate description of the property so that the guests can experience a true reflection of what they see in the photos. Bad reviews often stem from guests living in homes where the hosts are not truthful in their description.

Try to get the attention of your guests in the description headline. Use descriptive words that are catchy, friendly, and appropriate. Most people, for example, will respond better to *Amazing Disneyland Home* than a *One-Bedroom House for Rent*.

Airbnb allows you thirty-five characters in the description header, so use this wisely. You can try different title ideas until you settle on one that increases clicks and inquiries. Keep it short and catchy. Consider the audience you are targeting and the things that may appeal to them, and factor this into your description.

Credible description

A good description must be detailed. Ensure it is as accurate as possible. If there are unique features that make your home stand out from the rest, highlight this. It is also wise to let your guests know how many people can be hosted in your home.

Do you have additional services that can be offered at a fee, like laundry services? Make sure that you mention this. If you are aware of any constraints that they need to be aware of, like perhaps a slow internet connection, make sure you let them know.

Another area that is important but that most hosts neglect is the guest access segment. Most hosts use this to indicate how to access the premise, but that is not what it was intended for. The guest access area should indicate the facilities that your guests will enjoy in the premise, like a Jacuzzi, private pool or perhaps a special admission into a unique facility in the city, courtesy of your reputation.

Should any part of your premise have restricted access, ensure you let the guests know ahead of time.

Guest interaction

Your guests are on holiday and need their privacy. Given that, you need to be present without making your presence felt. Make yourself available for your guests whenever they need you. Other than that, do not bother them.

Provide a communication line so that you can promptly answer any questions they may have. Guests need an assurance that you will always be present if and when they need you, or organize for someone to promptly help with any concerns they may have. In case you are not available, let them know how they can get in touch with you.

Neighboring sights

The neighborhood may be a good way to sell your property online. Describe where the property is situated, and any important places that may be worth checking out. If your audience is a young and hip crowd, they would appreciate a list of awesome hangout spots that they can visit.

Airbnb ranking secrets

As an Airbnb host, one of your prime desires is to make sure your property ranks well compared to most of the other properties in your area. What most people are not aware of is that the search engine that powers Airbnb works in pretty much the same way that the Google search engine works.

The listings use the same algorithm, which means that the more times your listing shows up at the top of a user's query, the higher the chances that you will get a booking. Improving your ranking on Airbnb is very easy, but only if you do it right.

Creating a standout listing

For any listing to get attention from prospective guests, it must stand out, as people are always looking for properties that stand out and offer impressive quality. In the mind of a prospective guest, a responsive host is a good sign, and chances are, they will have an amazing time in your property.

When posting a listing, ensure you complete all sections, providing as much information as possible. Your guests only have one shot at falling in love with your property, so make sure they have all the information they need to make up their minds.

Completing all the necessary information in your listing will go a long way because it helps the guests know what they can look forward to. You can provide a detailed, informative and attractive description that explains what makes your property different from others and what makes it special. If you have special rules that the guests must be aware of, ensure to highlight this too.

Take quality photos and make use of proper lighting. Most people edit their photos to make them look better, but in the process, they only end up making them look fake. The right amount of light and angle can make a big difference for your photos.

A responsive host

Most people on Airbnb who ask questions about a listing are looking to confirm their booking almost immediately or are comparing between homes. Guests appreciate a host that responds to their messages almost immediately, or in a few minutes. Engage the guest as soon as possible. It is extremely frustrating to message a host and get a response days or weeks later, or in some cases never at all. It is good practice to respond to queries from guests as soon as you can in order to provide them with relevant information so that they can decide on the best property for their stay.

Imagine how amazing it is for a guest to come across a host who has a 100 percent response rate. This is a confidence boost, and they may overlook any other property that they may have been considering.

Besides, the Airbnb algorithm gives a better chance of listing homes with responsive hosts. Given that you may be a busy person, it is wise to have the Airbnb app installed on your phone so that you can respond to guest messages as soon as you receive them. You can also set it on Instant Book so that you can appeal to guests who seek last minute bookings. Instant book also improves your response rate and time.

Reviews

The service industry is powered by many things, and one of the most important is reviews. Reviews tell a story of your property from the perspective of guests who have lived there. If they had an amazing experience, anyone who reads your reviews would know. If something was off about your home, they could also write it in the reviews.

While hosts can spurn a few lies in the description of their properties, guests can fact check this and give a true picture of their experience in the review section. The more 5-star reviews you get, the better your property will be ranked, and your profile as a host will improve.

Do not be afraid of negative reviews; these happen all the time, even to the most amazing hosts. There will always be a guest who is very difficult to please or one who did not read your description and came in with a different expectation from what you explicitly described online. Some guests are just negative, and you cannot do anything about it. However, when you get legitimate bad reviews, you can use them as a learning point to discover the things that you can do to improve your home and make it more appealing.

Wish lists

Someone who is casually browsing on Airbnb and looking at options for a future date will want to save your property on their wish list. Even if your listing is not booked, adding it to a wish list is a sign that people are interested in it and may book it sometime in the future. This is good for your reputation.

Airbnb pricing strategies

It is not easy to set the right price for your property. You may worry about setting it too high or so low that you barely break even. Sadly, with Airbnb, there is no easy way to handle price. Each experience is unique, and therefore, the same applies to pricing. A lot of factors come into play when setting the right price, and for this reason, you have to be very careful about how to blend the factors together. The following are some factors that you need to consider when setting the ideal price for your property.

Determine the target guest audience

Who are you targeting with your listing? Answering this question can help you narrow down the expected traits of your guests and determine what they may be willing to pay for a listing like yours.

For example, think about the work that they do. If your listing may appeal to students, you need to think along the lines of affordable rates. If you are looking at professionals and business-minded people, research on appropriate rates for such guests.

You must spend a lot of time on research, or you will end up pricing your property out of range of your target audience. Another risk is setting the price so low that you are barely getting profits after meeting your regular expense allocation.

Hierarchical cost strategy

Have you ever noticed how new businesses come into the market with introductory offers, discounts, and the like? Some even give away their products and services at amazing rates. The same can apply with Airbnb.

For a new listing, your target is to get good reviews and a lot of attention. With this in mind, set your cost relatively low after researching what similar listings in your neighborhood cost. This will help you get a number of bookings in and, depending on how awesome your home is, good reviews too.

This will also give you an opportunity to learn from some of the first guests that you have. Think about their experiences, what they look forward to, and after a while, you will have a guest profile that can help you restructure your cost accordingly. Some guests become so loyal that they reach out to you directly and inform you of their plans to use your property again, so you can lock their preferred dates out of your Airbnb calendar. Over time, you can increase the cost accordingly.

Cost projections

One of the important factors that you must consider when setting the price for your property is the cost to keep it running. Maintenance expenses should never be ignored. Some of the other costs include things like supplies, licenses, transport costs, venue costs, permits, refreshments, and so on. List down all the things that you will have to spend on. You can save money by buying some of them in bulk.

Shun desperation

It may take a while before your property gets the attention you want, but this does not mean that you should sell yourself short. Desperation can make you undervalue your property in a bid to get guests streaming in. You may also attract troublesome guests in the process. Be patient and appreciate the value of your home.

Guest demographics

You can use the normal Airbnb statistics to determine the demographics of guests who may visit your property. In Europe and the US, most of the people who use Airbnb are between twenty-five and thirty-four years old. Also, most people spend at least two nights in premises located in urban centers. These statistics are available in the public domain and can help make a difference in the way you manage your property.

The type of property

Another important factor that will determine what you charge is the type of property you are letting. Luxury properties attract luxury prices. Another factor loosely related to your property which affects the price is your proximity to important points of interest like restaurants, sightseeing spots, and so on.

It is advisable that you adjust the price of your property accordingly so that guests appreciate the value on the price they are paying to use your property.

Study the competition

Keeping an eye on the market will not just help you set your price but can also serve as research to see how other hosts vary theirs. Take note of any events and holidays that may take place around the price change, and notice how their prices change in response to that.

Optimizing your photos for maximum bookings

Did you know you could be missing out on profits from bookings because of terrible photos on Airbnb? Take a look at some of the top-rated Airbnb listings. You will notice they all have amazing photos.

Before you take photos of the house, assume you already have a guest coming in. Arrange items in the house in preparation for their arrival. The perfect setting will help you manage guest expectations when they see your photos online. More importantly, make sure your house is clean and looking neat. The following are useful tips that can help ensure you have great photos for your property.

Proper light setting

Light helps accentuate the colors, depth, and natural contrast of your home. When taking photos during the day, turn on the lights. The great thing about awesome lighting is that it can help you make a normal smartphone photo look extremely professional. Before a daytime photo shoot, make sure you have the curtains and window blinds open to allow natural light in.

Why do you need to turn on indoor lights during the day? Overlook the issue of energy conservation for a minute and think about aesthetics. Turning the lights on will help you bring more light to the dimly lit corners, in the process providing a good idea of how great your property is. Besides, turning the lights on also shows people that you have a clean home.

Corner shots

Amateur homeowners take shots of their homes against flat walls. Experts, on the other hand, shoot corners of their homes. What is the difference between the two? A corner shot will add an element of dimensionality to your Airbnb photoshoot. Also, they bring the element of perspective into focus and can make your rooms look larger than they are.

Detail in the photos

Often, people who focus so much on the most important amenities in their homes forget about tiny details that actually matter. Some guests have a keen eye and will notice the small things that you overlook in your photos. Focus on things that give your home a personal touch and a welcoming presence for anyone who is looking for a getaway.

Using panoramic shots

A popular way of taking shots of the whole room in one simple photo is to use panoramic shots. Panoramic shots cover a wide angle. If you cannot take panoramic shots, get a wide-angle lens. Such shots are perfect as they show the size of your home and provide an element of trust. Guests can see the entire room, so they are comfortable that you are not hiding anything.

Lifestyle photos

Your photos should allow your home to ooze with personality and make it stand out. This is particularly true if you have a unique target audience for your property. Where necessary, show shots of the outdoors and the safety gear for cycling or kayaking, for example. Make sure that you show things that guests can appreciate and use.

If you are a very social and diverse individual, you can show as many things as you can, especially if your aim is to appeal to a wide variety of guests.

Local sites

Spend some time in town and take photos of some of the important sights that guests may want to check out. Photos of your neighborhood can give a rough idea of what they can look forward to. This works, especially for families who will appreciate a wide lawn for the children to play on or the beachfront.

Angular shots

Have you ever gone through an Airbnb listing to find photos taken only from one angle? This shows your home in a very boring and monotonous way. Try to take photos from all angles, as this is captivating and allows you to capture all the amenities in the house in incredible angles, and the artistry will probably get you more bookings.

Aspect ratio and resolution

You may have taken some amazing photos, but the resolution is not high enough. This is almost as bad as taking bad photos. Invest in a good camera. These days a good smartphone can work just as well.

Having low-quality, blurry photos sends the wrong message to your guests. It means that either you do not care about their experience or you do not care about your home, and none of these is good for business.

Airbnb recommends photo resolutions of at least 1024 × 683 pixels. If your camera can do better, go ahead. Ensure you upload photos with a width to length aspect ratio of 3:2. This is wise, because Airbnb automatically adjusts photos to suit the user's experience in terms of location and internet speed. Any other aspect ratio could be distorted when the photos are adjusted.

Chapter 9: Guest Relations

Messaging templates to communicate with guests

One of the most important things you need to do for your guest is communicate with them properly. You need to manage interactions and keep communication timely. To make things easier, a lot of hosts these days have message templates that they send to guests when they arrive. The templates save you time and help you interact with your guests. Here are some examples of templates that you can use when communicating with your guests:

>Template: Welcoming message before they arrive
>
>Hello (guest name).
>
>Thank you for your booking with us.
>
>I will send over useful information on the day you arrive.
>
>In the meantime, feel free to ask any questions so I can help you have a memorable stay.
>
>Do you have a special arrival request? Let us know so we can prepare adequately for you.
>
>Looking forward to hosting you.

(Host name)

Template: Checking up on the guest when they are in your premise

Hi (guest name).

I hope your first night in (location) is up to your expectations.

Did you settle in perfectly?

If there is something I can do to make your stay better and more enjoyable, do not hesitate to get in touch.

Thank you.

(Host name)

Template: Appreciation message when the guest has checked out of your premise

(Guest name),

We are grateful for having the pleasure of hosting you in our home.

Thank you for leaving our place so tidy and nice. It means a lot to us.

We had an amazing time hosting you, and we look forward to meeting you again soon.

Thank you.

(Host name)

My rules, my house

Having guests in your premise is an amazing feeling. You are finally getting people to book your property, and you are looking forward to earnings. However, without rules and regulations, things can quickly go south.

You need to set clear rules and communicate them with your guests. Some of the things you can mention include limiting smoking or highlighting the parts of the property that they do not have access to. Are your guests allowed to have visitors in the premise? Highlight this so that you do not end up in confrontations with your guests.

To edit or add rules for your home, go to the Your Listings page on Airbnb. Then, click on Manage Listing on the specific listing for which you want to add rules. Go to Booking Settings on top of the page. You should see the tab House Rules. Finally, click on it and edit.

Write the rules you need your guests to follow and then when you are done, save them. All the house rules mentioned will be visible on the listing page. Airbnb makes sure that guests review and agree to the rules before they can reserve a booking. As soon as the listing is booked, Airbnb will send the guest the rules. This way, they cannot claim to have never seen the rules when they are in contravention, and you take necessary action against them.

How do you make sure you highlight rules that do not deter your guests from having a good time in the house? First, remember that your guest is booking your home to have a good time and enjoy uninterrupted peace. Therefore, even if you come up with rules that have to be followed, you must make sure that they are not so strict that it feels like you are policing the guest.

When you are come up with house rules, make sure they are things that are not trivial but important to you. It is very easy for guests to overlook or break the rules when they are ambiguous or seem unnecessary. This is why you should come up with a list, and then narrow down the rules to the important things. Some things are a matter of common sense, but you can mention them as a reminder.

When writing your rules, keep things simple, and use plain language. No one wants a long list of things that they cannot do in your premise. Instead of explaining a lot of things in the rules section, you can show the guest around when they arrive and explain some things to them. This also gives them time to seek clarification. On average, you should list five to ten rules in the house book.

It is your home, but it is all about the guest and their holiday. With experience, you will know how to profile guests and identify the type of guests that you attract. With this in mind, come up with rules that are simple and easier for that demographic to follow.

Also, leave the house rules in a place that the guests can easily see and read them. Access makes a big difference and helps you make sure the guests are happy and following the set rules.

What happens if the rules are not followed or if there are damages? How do you handle it? Highlight a strategy that you share with your guests so that they are fully aware of the procedure. In some cases, you can deduct the damage cost from their security deposit.

Identifying problem guests before they book

There are different ways for you to identify problem guests. Problem guests often give you a difficult time and will end up giving you poor reviews even when they were in contravention of the basic rules that you shared with them.

Most of the information you need about a guest is on their profile. If they have at least three reviews as a host or a guest over a twelve-month period, there is a good chance that they are a good person.

You have to study their profile to look for alarming signs. Guests that have a very distasteful or hateful description should get your alarm bells ringing. Be careful with guests whose profiles are not close-up or not clear.

Look at their previous reviews. If the hosts write bad reviews about them, there is a good chance you will have a bad experience with them too. You should also be careful about guests who only have a single letter on their names. More often than not, these are made-up profiles.

Before you accept a booking, you are free to ask to know more about the guest. Airbnb takes things a notch higher by requesting guests to complete their profiles and verify their IDs. If you ask about the incomplete profile, problem guests always respond with something along the lines of being in a hurry, and they will complete their profile as soon as they are home.

Another thing that you can pay attention to is communication. Read between the lines and know a guest better. There is so much that you can tell about a person from the way they write. Short messages should get you concerned, so ask more questions to see if you can get the guest to respond better. If not, you are free to reject their reservation.

You must also be considerate in the way you approach this, given that more than 35 percent of Airbnb bookings are usually made by new guests. Many such guests do not have reviews. Therefore, you can ask them to complete their profiles politely.

Handling early arrivals and late checkouts

Having guests who arrive early or who checkout later than you expect can cause a lot of disruption. However, if it is an understandable reason, you can find a way to manage this and keep your guests happy. More often than not, early arrival or late checkouts can happen because of reasons that the guest has no control over.

It is safer not to offer early arrivals on your listing page directly. This is a good way to make sure that you do not have to stress yourself over clashing schedules. You must mention the desired check-in time on your listing so that you do not find yourself responding to late night arrivals.

Another option for you would be to get smart locks that allow the guest to check in remotely so that they can do so at whatever time they arrive. The same applies when they are checking out. If you allow your guests to check out later than your listing, ensure you highlight this and make sure they are aware of any additional costs where applicable.

Any guest who travels to your premise will have luggage. Whether they arrive early or are checking out late, you need to find a way to take care of this luggage. These are instances where you will have to be more concerned than strict. In case you are away, you can create a storage bin with a combination padlock on the property in a safe place that they have access to.

Dealing with Guest Cancellations

You may be familiar with the hotel cancellation policy. On Airbnb, the cancellation policy is different. You must study it and understand how it works. There are three basic cancellation policies that apply on Airbnb:

- *Flexible*—guest gets a full refund if they cancel a day before they arrive, minus the fees.

- *Moderate*—guest gets a full refund if they cancel five days before they arrive, minus the fees.

- *Strict*—guest gets a 50 percent refund if they cancel up to one week before they arrive, minus the fees.

Most of the listings on Airbnb have a strict cancellation policy. Therefore, even if you were to cancel your listing six months ahead of time, you will only get half of your total booking refunded.

This is aimed at protecting the hosts, given that getting a house booked on short notice and at very low prices is not easy. Many new hosts usually start their listings with flexible cancellation policies, and then from there, they can work things up to moderate or strict cancellation. According to Airbnb statistics, only around 3 percent of expert hosts have a flexible cancellation policy on their properties.

There are instances where Airbnb may choose to cancel the booking and refund the guest, and you should be aware of those. If the guest realizes that your home is not what is advertised, they can claim a refund and cancel the booking.

If your guest arrives and they are unable to access your listing, Airbnb cancels the reservation and offers them a full refund. This also applies if you do not respond to the guest on time.

If the guest arrives and notices that your property is not safe to live in, they can raise the issue with Airbnb, and the booking will be canceled, earning them a full refund. However, take note that the property must be proven unsafe—for example, if a guest is complaining about the presence of an animal in a property without it ever having been mentioned when they made their booking. For general issues or minor dissatisfaction claims, Airbnb does not cancel reservations.

When you cannot agree with the guest, the Airbnb Resolution Center can step in. The resolution team offers a mediation service in case you are unable to agree on how to proceed with cancellation. Before you cancel a guest's reservation, you must provide a good reason. A valid reason will enable Airbnb enough time to cancel the reservation without getting a bad review or a cash penalty.

Cancellations that are made within a week are charged one hundred dollars, while cancellations that are made at least seven days before the reservation is due are charged fifty dollars. In the case of a valid emergency cancellation, the resolution center will remove the cancellation fee and negative remarks that may have been listed on your account.

What to do if guests break something?

Every homeowner worries about the security of their premise when they are away. If you have breakable items in the house, you may worry that the guests do not take good care of them. However, there are items that you may not be able to remove always.

In such cases, if something breaks, you have fourteen days to raise a claim in the resolution center after the guest checks out or before your next guest checks in. In the resolution center, choose Request Compensation for Damages and provide details about the property that was damaged and any costs that are associated with it.

The Airbnb team will consult the guest, and if they agree to meet the cost, you will get a payout in five to seven working days. If the guest ignores the request or does not respond in seventy-two hours, you can click on Involve Airbnb, and they will take it up and resolve the issue in a week.

How to handle guests sneaking other people in

Your listing explicitly indicates the number of people who can be allowed into the house. If your home can accommodate more people, send the guest a change request which includes the nightly cost for each additional guest in the house.

If your home cannot support all the additional guests, inform the guest that your home is not suitable for them, and request that they cancel the reservation. Reservations canceled in this manner are refunded as per the cancellation policy you have in your premise.

How to consistently get five-star experiences from guests

If you want to get five-star recommendations from your guests, you must go the extra mile. Therefore, ensure you offer the guest an amazing stay. From the moment they book your property to the time they check in, make sure things are smooth and seamless.

Some things are not in your control, like the location of your home. What you can do is ensure that you communicate with the guest properly so that they understand where they are going.

Communication plays an important role in providing the guests with a good experience. Make sure you manage the guest's expectation so that they are not surprised when they come to your home. Given that your guests overlooked lots of other properties and selected yours, it is wise to make sure that they feel comfortable and appreciated.

As soon as the guest books your home, send them a warm and welcoming confirmation message. This message should include important details or information that they need when they check in. Avoid sending a very long instruction manual or constantly harassing them with messages.

Before they arrive, provide the guests with useful information. Your pre-arrival email should include the following:

- Direction and any special instruction to help your guests get to your home.

- Request detailed information so that you can get their residence prepared ahead of time for their check-in.

- Weather forecast information for the duration of their stay.

- Ask for any special requests the guest may have.

- Offer additional services to make their stay convenient.

These are simple things that you can go out of your way and do for your guest to ensure that they have the best possible time in your home.

Chapter 10: Automating the Airbnb Process

Most aspects of life today are automated, as it makes work easy for you and your guests. You do not have to run around doing mundane tasks, as they can be programmed to run on their own, on cue. As a property manager, automating your Airbnb rental will help you stay ahead of the pack. The following are some useful tips to automate your Airbnb rental.

Automated check-in

Property owners currently have electronic keys, and to access these keys, all you need is an electronic code. The beauty of electronic codes is that once a guest vacates the premise, you can always change the code to something else. It works like a password. You do not need to keep rekeying the premise or getting a new lock each time a guest leaves, for security purposes.

With a smart lock, most of the challenges you would have experienced with keys are a thing of the past. You are also in complete control of access to the premise. These also allow you to grant access to the premise remotely. If you manage many properties, you can use a security company that allows you to open one account, from where you can manage hundreds of keys. You will immediately receive a notification once a guest picks up the access code for your premise.

Using Airbnb management software

Property management companies have been using management software to automate their businesses for years. As an Airbnb property manager, you should also follow suit. A property management software allows you to monitor your bookings and anything else that is important to you through messages. Some of the things you can do with property management software at the click of a button include scheduling cleaning services, communicating with your guests, and managing the review system.

Property management software is a great idea, especially if you manage lots of properties on Airbnb. The following are some of the benefits you can get from it:

Guest communication

As an Airbnb property manager, it is important to stay in contact with your guests throughout the duration of their stay. This helps you handle any issues they have as they arise. Guests love a property manager who responds to their concerns in real time.

Other than addressing their concerns, a great communication platform would also allow you to preset specific messages at a given duration. These can be handy guides, plans, and tips that would make your guest's stay hassle-free.

On your part, make sure you choose a communication platform that sends you notifications immediately when your guest needs something. This way, you can swiftly respond to guest concerns, irrespective of the time, or where you are.

A great communication platform creates a beautiful environment for your guests. This also helps you establish a good rapport with them, which will, in the long run, increase your guest retention rates. Most of your guests will become regulars.

Managing multiple listings

An ideal property management software should support multiple listings. With this program, you synchronize different calendars in one interface, allowing you to manage all your Airbnb listings in one place. Whether you are getting guests from Booking.com, TripAdvisor, or whichever source, keeping your calendar synched will simplify your work.

Schedule cleaning services

With scheduled cleaning services, property management goes a notch higher. Everyone loves a residence that is fresh, clean, and presentable and has the aura of a perfect holiday. These are some of the things that people remember whenever they think of your property.

To manage the cleaning services, the right property management software creates a working schedule for your cleaning staff. They know what is supposed to be done and at what time. You can also set permissions so that each individual can only get access to specific work orders or tasks that you deem fit.

This is appropriate, especially when cleaning and other support services are needed when you have a guest checked in, and the guest requests this specific service. You can create cleaning tasks as per the guest's requirements and assign the roles accordingly.

Team management

Airbnb automation does not just end at cleaning services; you can take it a notch higher and automate your entire team. Support staff is just as important to your guest's stay as having an ideal premise, so each person on your team should have their tasks automated.

For example, the moment a customer confirms a booking, you can schedule someone to pick them up at the airport, if that option is available. You can create permissions for your staff based on the roles you need them to play from the time your guest confirms their booking, to the moment they check out of your property.

While it is easy to see the usefulness in automating Airbnb processes, automation should never replace the physical, hard work that is needed to keep the premise up to standard. Automation simply eliminates inconsistencies and inefficiencies and makes your business run smoothly. There are lots of automation programs out there for your Airbnb business. In due diligence, read about them, read the reviews from property managers who have used them, and try their free services before you upgrade to premium services.

Automation tools for Airbnb

It is now easier for you to streamline some of the repetitive tasks on Airbnb through automation, saving you time and money in the process. As an entrepreneur, you must make sure that every day, you want to provide them with an amazing experience. Managing your Airbnb property requires you to make sure the guest is satisfied and happy without being in their presence all the time. The following are some useful tools that will make your work easier.

Auto message

You can create a set of programmed messages that are custom-made for your guests. The messages are sent out at specific intervals during the day. Many tools currently support this functionality, and you can interact with the guests through email, text messaging, and other social media communication platforms like WhatsApp and Viber.

Automatic replies

A high response rate is one of the things that determine

whether you are a successful entrepreneur on Airbnb. With the right tools, you instantly send replies the moment a guest books your property. Prompt responses will make it easier for your guests to appreciate your input and improve your listings' rankings online.

Automatic reviews

Automatic reviews will help you improve your profile online. Chances are high that a guest who had an awesome stay in your property will leave you a good review. Therefore, it is only fair that you do the same for them. There are tools like Hosty that offer automatic reviews. Also, you can create personalized reviews for each guest who checks into your property. Worried about writing the same review all the time? No need to. Simply write a personal reply and the app will handle the rest for you.

Increasing efficiency as an Airbnb host

Many people are of the opinion that Airbnb automation is only useful for big companies, but this is far from the truth. You can automate your listing as an individual host to make it more efficient and improve the experience of your guests. Automation is all about creating a repeat sequence that handles the things you need to do like responding to emails and any other stuff that you may have previously had to handle manually.

The following are some of the safest ways to automate the Airbnb process, making it more efficient for you and your guests.

Automatic sensors

Sensors are important as they can help you automate routine activities in your home. A motion-triggered sensor is perfect for turning lights on and off, which means you will no longer have to spend a lot of money on electricity bills.

You should also have a smoke detector, water-leak sensor, and a carbon-monoxide sensor to determine whether your property is at risk, which could lead to an emergency situation. These sensors are programmable and can be linked to your communication devices, alerting you when something is not right.

Automated emails

Every host knows the importance of proper communication with guests. Prompt responses will improve your customer service rating, and they give you a better chance of interacting with the guest. Autoresponders are useful for this as they can help you overcome the stress of having to follow up on emails and respond to them one by one.

Some of the information that you can include in automated emails includes wireless network passwords, policies for checking in and checking out, directions to your property, and instructions for the exchange of keys when applicable. If you are using automated emails, it is wise to personalize the messages so that they address each guest personally without mistaking any of your guests.

Chapter 11: Scaling It Up to Six Figures or More

Airbnb has created opportunities for growth, and many entrepreneurs are currently earning a tidy sum off the platform. Many have even quit their day jobs to focus on increasing their listings on Airbnb.

What makes these entrepreneurs different from other individuals, and how are they able to earn good profits? There are more than seventy people who earn over $1 million in income from Airbnb every year. How do they do it? What can you learn from this to raise your earnings?

According to relevant information in the industry, the cities with the highest earnings are Sydney, Havana, Cape Town, Bali, and London. London is such a high-earning place that one landlord raked in more than £11 million in one year by leasing out more than 800 properties.

Given this growth trajectory, it is easy to see that Airbnb has evolved into a place where you can create a business empire and create other jobs for people who help clean and manage the properties. Airbnb has created a secondary market from the property-listing market, and it is thriving with opportunities.

What skills set these hosts apart from other individuals and what can you learn from them to boost your potential on Airbnb? Here are some of the things that will get you there:

Winning mentality

If you were to sit down with any of the people who have had success on Airbnb, one thing that you will learn from them is that they have a passionate desire to be wealthy and succeed in life. These are people who want to create a lot of wealth. Success inspires them to strive for more.

When you have a winning mentality, you are always looking for ways to better manage your business and keep things running smoothly so that you generate more income without spending too much. To achieve this, most, if not all, of these entrepreneurs have automated their Airbnb process.

There are professional property and Airbnb management systems that can make your work easier, saving you time and money on random activities that need be carried out. Outsource other tasks like maintenance and cleaning and keep them on a schedule. This allows you room to monitor costs and keep your business growing.

Importance of multiple listings

More than 75 percent of Airbnb hosts only have one listing. While it is okay to start small and work with what you have, if you want to succeed and earn a good sum on Airbnb, you must think about multiple listings. Multiple listings in different locations allow you to spread your risk exposure, and having a diverse portfolio will allow you to earn every month of the year, regardless of whether some cities are trendy or not.

Apt business mind-set

To help you succeed with an Airbnb listing, you must also have a business mind-set. Airbnb is more than just about listing properties. More than 75 percent of properties on Airbnb earn less than $10,000 a year. On the other hand, the top entrepreneurs on Airbnb earn a very good amount, raking in money from most of the bookings that are made on Airbnb on a daily basis. Statistics from Airbnb indicate that the leading entrepreneurs only make up 8 percent of the total listings on Airbnb, but on average they take home more than 18 percent of the booking revenues earned on the platform.

How do they do this? The entrepreneurs have good business acumen and can operate their listings in the most efficient manner. They have teams in place with specific roles, and all these are outlined down to a system that works efficiently.

Perfect imperfections

A lot of hosts worry about ratings, especially if they cannot get five-star ones. Do not be blinded by the desire to get five-star ratings, as studies have shown that guests do not always opt for listings that have five-star ratings. Most people look for ratings above four stars but not a complete five. Listings with 4.5-star rating are among the properties that bring in the most revenue on Airbnb.

Location choice

If you want to succeed with Airbnb, choose your location, because not all locations can bring in a lot of money. Even in cities like London and Sydney, there are prime locations that are an Airbnb entrepreneur's paradise and others that barely get any attention. More than half of the revenue earnings on Airbnb are attributed to the presence of a home in a desirable location.

This is not a difficult thing to achieve, considering that a beach house with an ocean view, for example, will get more attention and views online than a simple house in a suburb somewhere in the city. Your real estate choices will go a long way in determining how far you can go with your Airbnb project.

Risk management

Like any other business, there is risk involved in Airbnb. To succeed, you must learn how to mitigate risks and minimize your exposure. Most of the expert entrepreneurs are very good at identifying bad guests. These are the people who show up to your property with a bad attitude, damage your property, cause havoc and disturb the neighborhood but give you a bad rating when, in response, you take stern action or act according to the law.

It is safer to create a guideline for the kind of guests that you introduce to your property. It is important that you address the guidelines and make them clear so that you can avoid interacting with guests who do not meet your standards. The fewer problems you have with your guests, the easier it will be for you to maintain good standing and status as a Superhost, who are the top earners on Airbnb.

Sound business plan

Do you have a business plan, or are you just going around randomly hosting people? You may have started out small, but you need to have a plan in place to grow your business. Most hosts treat Airbnb like a side hustle, ignoring its full potential. If you want to succeed with Airbnb, make sure you plan properly and treat this business as you would any other.

A lot of the top earners on Airbnb are listed as professional property management companies. You need to follow this model and make sure you give the venture the professional attention it needs in regards to management and operations.

Chapter 12: Advanced Airbnb Tips

Save money on linens, towels, and sheets: How to prevent guests from staining your towels and sheets

Worried about constantly spending money replacing sheets, towels, and linens? You can tackle this issue in the house rules section. Simply put up simple instructions for your guests that they can follow when they are in your house. Indicate a separate setting for makeup, facial medication, whitening toothpaste, tanning products, and anything else that may require special attention.

Before you confirm the reservation request, ensure the guest has read the house rules. You can politely ask them to confirm whether they have, and if not, encourage them to do so. Simple things in the house rules can make a difference in whether you will enjoy hosting them or not.

How much should you pay your property managers?

When listing the property on Airbnb, professional property management is something you have to consider. A property manager is an individual or a company that will take care of your property. Each property manager has a set of terms and conditions and costs that come with their services, so you must research well to find one that is suitable for your property and your budget.

Some of the roles of a property manager include making sure that the property is clean and in good condition for the next guest, as well as organizing airport pick-ups and drop-offs upon the guest's request. Some property managers are so advanced that they even offer legal services like taxes and any other documentation that you may need.

It is not easy to tell what the average cost of property management will be on Airbnb. The reason for this is because all properties are unique, as are all the needs of each host. Each Airbnb market has unique features, and property managers will charge you depending on the features of the markets they operate in. Properties also have varying demand rates, occupancy rates and the duration of time the property stays unoccupied.

A property manager may be an additional cost, but a worthy one if you want to avoid the trauma that comes with managing multiple listings. For a single listing, you can easily handle the tasks that are involved in keeping the listing Airbnb ready.

Some of the things that property managers consider when setting the billing charge for your premise include the size of your property, the age of the property, the services that you want from them, and the location of the property.

Advice on bedding and sheets

There is so much more to setting up your Airbnb than simply

getting the perfect location. You must have taken some amazing photos and edited some of them, added some filters, polished them, and made them look great. However, it does not end there. What is inside the house makes a big difference in the guest's overall experience. Bedsheets, beddings, and pillows are some of the things that beginner hosts often overlook. Ask yourself whether the sheets you have are good enough or if you need a new set. Whatever decision you make, it all comes down to the cost of getting additional beddings.

Think about this as if you were furnishing your home. With the right settings and appliances, you can turn a house into paradise. Your guests are looking for the perfect place to forget about their normal lives for a while and enjoy some peace and quiet.

To create that aura, you need to focus on things that make your listing comfortable. Think about beds, beddings, pillows, and so on.

One of the first things that guests look at when they come to your home is the bedroom as they want to see where and how they will sleep. If someone is not comfortable with the sleeping arrangement, they will not be fully satisfied with their stay, however much effort you put into it.

Bedsheets should be at the top of your priority list. There are many ways to deal with bedsheets. You can choose to match them with the walls or with some other association in the house, giving off a cool and calm experience. Some colors are too noisy and will not be suitable for most holiday seekers.

Aside from the color, shop for quality bedsheets. After all, you are offering your guests a glimpse of paradise. Research and go to different stores, and look at the thread count, the material, the texture, and so forth. Settle on bedsheets that give off a royal feel. Spending on quality beddings is always a worthy investment.

You also need to find a balance between comfort, luxury, and price. Think about your bed, for example. Would you feel comfortable sleeping in the same beddings that you are providing to your guests? If not, move along and find something else. You must create a comfortable space in the house. It is advisable that you get new bedsheets for your guests, as most people do not like to sleep in the same beddings as strangers. If you have very expensive bedsheets, it is advisable not to use them for the Airbnb experience, unless you do not mind other people using them.

Given that, the following are some of the things you should consider when looking for quality bedsheets for your Airbnb listing:

- They should not have stains.
- They must be soft.
- There should not be any rips or tears.

Other than these, three important factors determine whether you have the right sheets for your Airbnb listing: the color, the material, and the thread count.

Color

Getting the right color of bedsheets is not always an easy task. Some people do it effortlessly, others struggle to get it right, while others never seem to know what they are doing. Your safest bet with bedsheet colors is to choose something that inspires a hotel look.

To get a rough idea, visit a few hotels and have a look at their bedsheets. Hotels prefer white sheets, as it is easier to bleach and clean them. Make peace with the fact that sheets will get stained; you just can't get around that.

If you are good with colors and prints, you can try printed sheets. Some hosts have been successful with dark-printed bedsheets too. It's all about what you feel comfortable with and the vibe you want your room to give off.

Material

Regarding the material, the same sentiments apply. Choose something you are comfortable with, and common options are silk and cotton sheets. You should choose the material for your bedsheets according to the clientele that you are targeting.

Thread count

You do not necessarily need to get some fine quality Italian or Egyptian cotton bedsheets. A six-hundred-thread bedsheet is a sure winner over a two-hundred-thread bedsheet, but do you really need to spend that much?

The decision comes down to what you are willing to spend. If you are comfortable buying pricey Egyptian bedsheets, go ahead. What you must prioritize, though, is the quality of the bedsheets. Even if you are not buying the Egyptian sheets, make sure you get something that will last for a long time and allow your guests to sleep well. Besides, hosting on Airbnb is also about first impressions.

At the same time, remember that you should also provide spare beddings, so in every bed in the house, provide at least two or three pairs of sheets. Everyone loves a backup plan. Assuming your Airbnb business picks up, and your listings come quick and fast, you may have someone checking in as soon as another checks out. Therefore, you will not have enough time to clean the sheets and get them ready for the next guest.

Having spare sheets will also help in case of a cleaning mishap, or if the sheets are stained. As your business grows, you can keep buying more. Having a spare set of sheets always gives you peace, knowing that you never have to worry about random emergency situations with guests.

Other than the bedsheets, the following are some of the other things you need to look at to make your guest's stay in your home amazing:

Bedbug covers

Having bedbug covers is a good way to keep your pillows and mattress safe. This is purely a maintenance concern. It is easier to wash the covers than the mattress and pillows. You can also shop around for covers that offer protection from accidental spills. Bedbug covers are available for as little as sixty dollars.

Pillows

What is the condition of your pillows? Assuming you were renting your property, would you be comfortable using the pillows that you are providing? Make sure you have pillows that are in good condition and not too flat. If they are flat, buy a new set. Also, you should never have sweat-stained pillows in your property. Many guests strip the bed and make it before they sleep in it, and finding stained pillows will earn you a bad rating.

Duvets and duvet coverlets

Depending on the color and patterns that you buy, duvets can make your bed look beautiful and peaceful. During the cold months, duvets provide additional warmth protection for your guests. There are different types of duvets that available in the market; you can choose from goose feather duvet or a hypoallergenic duvet, which are ideal for people who worry about allergies. Coverlets are recommended when the weather is warmer, as they are lighter, thinner, and more comfortable than duvets.

Conclusion

There are many reasons guests consider Airbnb over any other form of accommodation. If you are the host, it is up to you to make sure that the guest has a good time. You can do this by going out of your way to make sure their stay is uninterrupted and that they have a good time in your premise.

There is a lot more to Airbnb's appeal than the price, so you need to factor this into your plans for the property. Most people look for accommodation that can host a large group under one roof at the same time, instead of having to check into different hotel rooms. This is one of the perks of using Airbnb.

Airbnb offers a great opportunity for hosts and guests to learn more about one another and foster a relationship of trust. Most people are friendly and respect one another's privacy, as well as the house rules. However, there are always a few bad characters who manage to sneak through the Airbnb filters. These are rare experiences, but they can be addressed as they happen.

For a beginner host, I provided useful tips that will help you learn how to start your listing and increase the prospect of earning more in the process. Many of the top hosts on Airbnb started from humble beginnings, but with hard work and sheer determination, they made it to where they are today.

The real estate market is one where most people who are making good money are those who own property. However,

Airbnb is proof that you can make a lot of money from the market without owning any. You need to foster a strong relationship with your landlord for them to understand why it is a good idea to lease their property to be used on Airbnb. While this may seem like something you need do to get the landlord on board, your success becomes the landlord's success, and before you know it, the two of you can have a very productive business relationship.

A lot of good things have been said about Airbnb, and it is possible that this may cloud your judgment. Do not jump the gun. You need to work hard. Research well and study the market before you decide to invest in a given niche. Understand the demographics and the challenges that homeowners experience in specific markets. This is information that can help you turn a tidy profit from Airbnb by setting your business a notch higher than the competition.

The Airbnb journey is one that will get you places. If you are keen, you can make a big difference from the moment you list your first property on Airbnb to the moment you start raking in significant revenue from multiple listings. To make a significant impact, you will need multiple listings. However, do not rush. The learning curve on Airbnb is steady, and you should adhere to it. If you take on too much work at the same time, you may struggle to handle it well and end up losing sight of your core goals.

Don't Miss Out! Last Chance to FINALLY Solve This Problem!!

According to Cornell University, "Entrepreneurial activity depends on the decisions that people make, suggesting that the attributes of the decision makers should influence the entrepreneurial process."

97% of businesses fail because after a few hurdles which **EVERY** entrepreneur faces eventually, they get discouraged and lose their drive.

Download this **FREE** book to learn how you can avoid this nasty trap and be one of the successful 3%!

Hurry! Obtain the **best** mindset for yourself before it's too late!! Click on the link below and claim your FREE book on how:

http://bit.ly/SecretsForAirbnb

CPSIA information can be obtained
at www.ICGtesting.com
Printed in the USA
LVHW110452071222
734702LV00007B/296